THE ECONOMIC DEVELOPMENT OF
THE ITALIAN-AMERICAN

By

ROBERT J. WECHMAN, Ph. D.

Dept. of Business and Economics
BMCC, City University of New York
Pace University
St. Thomas Aquinas College

ISBN 0-87563-232-7

STIPES PUBLISHING COMPANY

Published By
STIPES PUBLISHING COMPANY
10 - 12 Chester Street
Champaign, Illinois 61820

To:

Stephanie

Craig

Evan

Darren

Table of Contents

Chapter I

THE ECONOMICS OF THE ITALIANS IN
THE UNITED STATES TILL 1870

The Italians were part of the earliest encounters with the land which became known as America. Christopher Columbus (Cristoforo Colombo) from Genoa landed in the Western Hemisphere in 1492. John Cabot (Giovanni Caboto), also from Genoa, was the discoverer of Nova Scotia, Labrador and Newfoundland. The name America comes from the Florentine explorer Amerigo Vespucci. The first European to discover New York Harbor was an Italian from Florence named Giovanni Verrazzano.

During the age of exploration, Italians served as missionaries and soldiers for France and Spain. Nicola Strozzi served as a Captain in the French army and was killed in 1565 in Florida in a battle with the Spaniards. Father Marco da Nizza settled in what is presently the State of Arizona in 1536. In 1610, some Italian craftsmen settled at Jamestown, Virginia in response to an invitation issued by the British settlement. Some of the Italians were winegrowers, most of them desiring land, moved from the Jamestown settlement and finally settled to the West, to the South and migrated to the settlements in New England. During the age of exploration one finds in New York City (then Nieuw Amsterdam) a number of successful Italians. "In 1655 we hear of one Mathys Capito, an Italian, who became clerk in the Municipal Bookkeeping Office. There were also a few Italian Jews, some of the Spanish-Portuguese stock, living in the city. Among the most prominent of these were: Salvatore d'Andradi, Abraham de Lucina, David Frere and Joseph d'Acosta, some of whose descendants became prominent businessmen in New York. By the end of the seventeenth century (1699) Antonio Crisafi, an Italian, held the vital military post of Governor of Fort Onondaga on the then western frontier of the Province of New York." (1)

In 1657 a group of Italians, professing the harshly persecuted Waldensian heresy, (2) immigrated from Piedmont, Italy, and settled in Delaware, near what is presently the town of New Castle. "It is believed...that some of these Waldensians established a settlement at Stony Brook, Staten Island, where they founded what is said to have been the first church of any denomination on the island. Nearly eighty years later another church of Waldensians, skilled in the culture of silkworms and vines, arrived and settled in Georgia, Virginia and South Carolina. Again, in 1768, a band of Italians, slightly more than one hundred in number, settled in Florida at what is now New Smyrna." (3)

Filippo Mazzei, was a distinguished scientist who settled in Jamestown, Virginia in 1773. He became a friend of George Washington, Benjamin Franklin and Thomas Jefferson and was among the earliest colonists who favored breaking off from England. By 1774, even though there were few Italians in the United States, they were in almost all aspects of the country's economic life. They operated stores in Florida, were fur traders on the frontier and ran blacksmith shops in New York City. (4) "Even in colonial days...some Italian musicians had begun to be active here. After the Revolution, they began to come in greater numbers, although it was not until 1814 that they arrived in a steady and noticeable stream. Just after the turn of the century, one Filippo Traetta founded the first conservatory of music in the country." (5) Italian painters and sculptors were not very prominent during the early days of the Republic. Constantino Brumidi, who was often called "the Michelangelo of the Capitol," was probably the most famous.

Unlike the Spanish and French, the English "sought the assistance of aliens in establishing and developing their colonies." In 1610, Virginia brought in European winegrowers, and by 1622 "had sent for a small group of Venetians in a futile attempt to save a moribund glass works and silk industry." Maryland passed a law in 1648 encouraging French, Dutch and Italians to settle there. In 1649, the Toleration Act was passed, giving Catholics religious freedom. Italian Jesuits and other clergymen soon "became active in spreading the gospel." Italian Protestants and Jews were welcomed in Georgia, the Carolinas and New Amsterdam. From the 16th Century, "Italians were active in Florida, as soldiers, sailors and missionaries with the conquistadors. When the British took over the Floridas in 1763, over 100 Italians, "apparently recruited from a group of wanderers in Leghorn, were attracted by the promise of land in America to Dr. Andrew Turnbyll's ill-fated colony at New Smyrna." The New Smyrna colony failed, and a large group of Italians and Greeks left the colony. The colony was abandoned completely in 1778, and many of its first settlers moved to St. Augustine, where they engaged in farming, hunting and fishing. Throughout the American colonies there were Italian weavers, cabinetmakers, gardeners, artists, musicians and businessmen. (6)

One of the most famous Italian priests to engage in North American missionary work was the Reverend Eusebio Fransisco Kino. Kino set up 24 missions in southern Arizona and northern Mexico between 1698 and 1711, introduced new varieties of grains and fruits, aided the Indians in the raising of livestock, mapped a large portion of this area, "and recorded many items of historical value in his memoirs." Reverend Kino "provided a base from which future cattle kings and fruit growers would build." (7)

A group of Vincentians, dominated at first by Italians, "played an important role in the history of the Catholic Church in early nineteenth century America." The original group, more than half of whom were Italians, left for America in 1816. They eventually established the first Roman Catholic seminary west of the Mississippi River (St. Mary's in Perryville, Missouri). Led by Neapolitan Giuseppe Rosati (later to become the first bishop of St. Louis), Italian missionaries helped build over thirty churches over a period of twenty years, and aided in establishing colleges, seminaries, academies, convents, an orphan asylum, a hospital, and one of America's first schools for deaf-mutes. "Italian priests were truly catholic in their labors, helping the faithful regardless of their nationality." There were few Italians to whom they could preach, in any case. Italians of other religious orders worked among the Indians, designed buildings for city and state governments in the Midwest, and "made substantial contributions to higher education." Such congregations founded Georgetown University, St. Bonaventure College and the College of Santa Clara. Italians helped to provide both faculty and administrators for these institutions. (8)

In New York City there were about twenty Italian families in 1790. "The medical and dental professions were adequately represented" by Dr. James Magro, who was practicing in 1765, by Dr. Orsi in 1789 (both physicians), and by Dr. G. Ruspini, a dentist who advertised himself in New York papers shortly after the Revolution as "the surgeon dentist to His Royal Highness, the Prince of Wales." Toward the close of the century, Louis Piris, an Italian surgeon dentist, began practicing in New York City. He claimed to minister to the poor free of charge. (9)

Several Italian singers, musicians and actors performed in New York during the late eighteenth century. On April 28, 1774, "a subscription concert was held for the benefit of Signora Mazzanti, who, it is thought, was the first Italian singer introduced to America." Later that year, Nicola Biferi of Naples arrived in New York to appear in concerts and teach voice, composition and harpsicord. "He opened what was probably the first school of music in New York." Signor Francheschini, "a conductor of considerable reputation," who had appeared in Philadelphia and Charleston, was honored at the close of the season for the year 1873 with a concert held by Loosley's Brooklyn Hall." Charles Ciceri of Milan painted the scenery for <u>Tammany</u>, a successful play which opened at the John Street Theatre in 1794. (10)

Italians in eighteenth century New York City also worked as magicians, painters, teachers, printers, liquor dealers, confectioners, restauranteurs, ice-men, ran boarding houses and carpenters. (11)

During the 1850s in California, trade and transportation were the only fields in which Italians accounted for over 1% of the workers. By 1870, however, agriculture and mining together accounted for more than 50% of working Italians. In the separate job categories, Italians were chiefly miners, agricultural laborers, fishermen, traders, dealers, hucksters, and peddlers. (12)

Merchants and retailers were also to be found among New York City's Italian community by the Civil War, but were outnumbered by Italian tailors, barbers, hairdressers, and laborers. As in Chicago, many Italians were artisans, and served as manufacturers of plaster images, interior decorators, cabinetmakers, bakers, carpenters, painters, stonecutters and musical-instrument makers. New York, unlike Chicago, had a large number of the famous Italian organ-grinders. Most numerous of all occupations "were the 160 professionals, the artists and musicians, who accounted for about one-third of the gainfully employed Italians in the city." (13)

During the 1850s, the number of Italians in the United States increased almost 300 percent--from 3,645 in 1850 to 10,518 in 1860. During this decade, 9,231 Italians arrived in the United States compared with 4,561 during the preceding 30 years. The Italians in 1860 still only represented 0.26 percent of the nation's total foreign-born population. They were, however, found in every state in the union, the largest con- centrations being as follows: California--2,805, New York--

1,862; Louisiana--1,134; Pennsylvania--622; Missouri--554; Ohio--407; and Tennessee--373. (14)

Picking the names of 100 Italians at random from Trow's New York City Directory for 1860, it was found the following trades or professions among those chosen: physicians-2, clerks-2, jewelers-2, manufacturers of barometers and thermometers-2, tailors-8, merchants-7, liquor, wines and beer-9, confectioners-3, cigars-3, musicians-6, artists-5, boots-5, barbers-3, cabinetmakers-3, plasterer and paper-hangings-2, statuary-3, flowers-3, and one each of the following- "carman, importer, coal agent, grocer, butcher, restauranteur, mason, hatter, broker, polisher, moulder, marble, painter, speculator, peddler, feathers, cutter, fruits, foundry, agents, mustard, riding, cooking, block cutter, seaman, manufacturer, drugs, professor, teacher, school, architect and lawyer." (15) During this period the Italian states had adopted a policy of deporting political prisoners to the United States. Many of the other Italians arriving in the United States were poor and unskilled. (16)

During the 1850s, in New York City's local affairs, Italians "played a rather insignificant role." In 1857, however, when a man named Cancemi was charged with murdering a police officer, the Italian population of the city rose in protest against a "feeling of hatred and revenge which had been manifested by a certain element of New York's population against all Italians in general. Some Italians of a very peaceable and highly honorable character were shamefully insulted and almost mobbed either in public thoroughfares, in their dwellings, or in their places of business." A committee of 17 prominent Italians "issued an appeal to the American public pointing out the injustice of holding the entire Italian community responsible for the isolated act of one individual...." The Italian group pointed out that statistical data from American courts revealed that Italians actually perpetrated less crimes in proportion to their total population in the United States than members of other immigrant groups, and that Italians were generally hard-working and of high moral character. (17)

There were several unsuccessful attempts by various companies to establish an Italian opera in the City of New York before 1850. In 1850-51 Marty's Havana Opera Company opened with the opera Norma. It attracted fine Italian singers, and "after another month of triumphs, on June 8, 1850, the Havana Company began to perform at Castle Garden where Norma continued to be one of the most popular offerings." Other Italian opera producers such as Maretzek, Barnum and Jaell achieved great success during the early 1850s. "On June 23, 1852, Marietta Alboni, unquestionably the greatest singer of mid-century, performed to a full house at Metropolitan Hall. She took the place that Jenny Lind had occupied in the hearts of New York music lovers." On December 27, 1852 Alboni appeared in her first opera in the United States at the Broadway Theatre as Cenerentola. "The Academy of Music at Irving Place, destined for over thirty years thereafter to be the home of opera in New York City, was opened on October 2, 1854, with Grist and Mario starring in the performance of Norma, their most successful offering." The first appearance in the United States of Verdi's Rigoletto was on February 19, 1855, Rossini's William Tell was first performed on April 9, 1854, and Verdi's Il Trouvatore on May 21, 1854. "The last, and perhaps the best known Italian actress of this decade, was Adelina Patti, who was described as the 'violet of all violettas,' and who appeared for the first time at the Academy of Music on November 24, 1859, Thanksgiving night. From that night on, ...she became the reigning queen of song, with none to dispute her leadership for more than thirty years." (18)

Italy participated in the New York Universal Exposition in 1853. "This evidenced the increasing prestige of Italy in the United States." Represented were Italy's arts and her industrial manufacturers. "The Austrian consul in New York had placed the mark 'Austria' on all objects coming from Lombardo-Venetia for the Universal Exposition. But the directors had the word 'Austria' changed to 'Italy', so that foreigners would know that Lombardo-Venetians were Italians and that the fact that Lombardy and Venetia were under the iron yoke of Austria, it did not imply that they were Croats." (19)

By 1850 trade between the United States and the Italian states, as well as the number of passengers who traveled back and forth, was so large that plans were begun for the establishment of a steamship line between Genoa and New York. Livingston Wells & Company announced plans to operate a steamship between the two cities. Negotiations between the United States and Sardinian governments were begun. They failed, however, despite Count Cavour's enthusiasm to start such a project. In 1852, Senator H. Fish presented a bill for the establishment of a line of steamers between New York and Genoa. This plan also failed. "On May 8, 1852, Mr. L. Mossi, the Sardinian charge in Washington, wrote to Count Cavour that the United States Congress was unwilling to appropriate money for the establishment of a line of steamers between New York and Genoa because it did not see the wisdom nor the need for this enterprise." The United States finally approved the formation of a trans-Atlantic navigation company. "Mr. Valerio, in a dispatch dated New York, August 3, 1853, to Count Cavour, stated that all the newspapers had written favorably of the enterprise, praising the Sardinian government for the support it had given to this company." (20)

During this period the Italians were also settling, though sparsely, in the West. Along with the Irish, Russians, Hungarians and Austrians, the Italians were a significant part of the labor force in the building of the railroads in the West. (21)

Italians also took part in the American Civil War. On April 27, 1861, L'Eco d'Italia outlined the organization of an Italian Legion (Legione Italiana) to help defend the union. The Legion was to be under the command of Italian officers. The newspaper La Nazione of Florence "commented favorably on this private initiative" and announced that Washington "extended a most cordial invitation to the former officers of Garibaldi to join the armies of the North, offering them generous and advantageous terms." Another regiment of Italians, organized by Colonel L.W. Tinelli, was known as the Garibaldi Guard. According to an editorial in the New York Herald, it included "all the organ-grinders of the city." It described them as "a hardy and enduring race, familiarized with hardship and exposure," and promised to "make excellent soldiers." Members of other national groups, including Frenchmen, Swiss, Spaniards and Hungarians soon joined the Garibaldi Guard, as did the Italian Legion. The Garibaldi Guard took part in the Battle of Bull Run, Siege of Harper's Ferry and the Battle of Gettysberg. (22)

During the greater segment of the nineteenth century, especially before Italy's unification in 1870, most of the Italians who emigrated from Italy went to South America rather than the United States. Most of the immigrants were from northern Italy and most went to Brazil and Argentina. However, after unification was achieved and legal restrictions were not enforced or were abolished, the exodus from southern Italy began.

Source Notes

(1)   Federal Writers Project, The Italians of New York (New York: Random House, 1938), p. 6.

(2)   The Waldensians were founded by Peter Waldo, a merchant of Lyons, France who C. 1173 gave up all his possessions to the poor and set about on a life of poverty. Eventually, Waldo and his followers developed an anti-cleric attitude and denied special priestly powers. Due to this they received the condemnation of the church.

(3)   Federal Writers Project, op. cit., pp. 6-7.

(4)   Lawrence Frank Pisani, The Italians in America (New York: Exposition Press, 1957), pp. 20-21.

(5)   Ibid., p. 36.

(6)   Luciano J. Iorizzo and Salvatore Mondello, The Italian American (New York: Twayne Publishers, Inc., 1971), pp. 10-11.

(7)   Ibid., p. 7.

(8)   Ibid., pp. 11-12.

(9)   Howard R. Marraro, "Italo-Americans in Eighteenth-Century New York," New York History, XXI, No. 2 (July, 1940), 316-318.

(10)   Ibid., p. 318.

(11)   Ibid., pp. 318-323.

(12)   Iorizzo and Mondello, op. cit., p. 13.

(13)   Ibid., pp. 13-14.

(14)   Howard R. Marraro, "Italians in New York in the Eighteen Fifties, Part I," New York History, XXX, 2 (April, 1949), 181.

(15)   Ibid., pp. 181-182.

(16)   Ibid., pp. 183-198.

(17)   Howard R. Marraro, "Italians in New York in the
           Eighteen Fifties, Part II," New York History,
           XXX, 3 (July, 1949), 289.

(18)   Ibid., pp. 290-294.

(19)   Ibid., p. 295.

(20)   Ibid., pp. 295-297.

(21)   Andrew Rolle, The Immigrant Upraised (Norman: The
           University of Oklahoma Press, 1968), p. 151.

(22)   Howard K. Marraro, "Lincoln's Italian Volunteers From
           New York," New York History, XXIV, 1 (January,
           1943), 56-66.

Chapter II

THE CONTRIBUTION OF ITALIAN MUTUAL BENEFIT
ORGANIZATIONS TO THE ECONOMIC DEVELOPMENT
OF THE ITALIAN IMMIGRANT

Italian mutual benefit societies played a very important role in the economic and social development of the Italian-Americans. They helped the new immigrant to the United States adjust in a variety of ways. They provided economic aid, business guidance, social and political help.

The earliest Italian societies in the United States were developed on the basis of town or province of birth. Italian organizations were set up to meet economic, social, or political needs. In general, the Italians did not look for economic aid from either local, state or national government. At times the membership of an Italian organization was limited to the residents of a particular street or building. Over the course of time small units consolidated into larger ones, and Italian heritage, rather than place of birth, became the chief criteria for joining. (1)

From the beginning, the village-mindedness of the Southern Italians was striking to American observers. When the immigrants settled in the blocks of New York or in the small industrial communities around the city, they tended to congregate with others from the same province or even village. Illiteracy seriously hampered the development of these diverse settlements into a single ethnic group, for differences in dialect, which in turn engendered mutual suspicion, tended to endure in the absence of widespread written communication. The Italian Press was hampered not only by the illiteracy of its clientele but also by the existence of a great gap between the ordinary spoken language and the official language of the press. (2)

The Italian government also helped the Italian immigrants in America. The Society for Italian Immigrants, tried to protect ignorant arrivals from thieves and swindlers and gave the immigrant food and shelter for 50 cents a day, till work could be found. This Society was subsidized by the Italian Government as they did the Home for Italian Immigrants which was established by the St. Raphael Society. The Italian government also maintained an Italian labor bureau in New York City to help in the distribution of immigration, and Italian immigrant inspectors notified the Italian government as to the conditions of labor in the United States. The Italian government also gave $60,000 toward the building of an Italian hospital in New York City. (3)

The Society for Italian Immigrants, which was incorporated in New York City in March, 1901 was the most influential organization for aiding the Italian poor during the early part of the twentieth century. Founded by the American reformed Sarah Wool Moore, with its first secretary Gino C. Speranza, "its great success rested upon the willingness of American reformers, Italo-American progressives, the Italian government and Italian citizens to cooperate in a concerted drive to uplift the Italian urban poor in America." The Society had representatives at Ellis Island assist Italian newcomers in locating relatives, buying railroad tickets, etc. As the Society's first headquarters on Pearl Street was too small to offer lodging, immigrants were sent to the Italian Benevolent Institute on Hancock Street if they did not have a place to live. In 1908, the Society was able to provide accommodations as well, and a new five-story building was erected which provided living quarters for 182 boarders. (4)

If, occasionally, an Italian immigrant could not find his relatives and did not have any money, he was placed in the Society's custody for one year. The Society gave the federal authorities "assurance that these foreigners would not become public charges." The Society for Italian Immigrants also maintained a labor bureau to find work for Italian immigrants outside of New York City and offered them protection against exploitative practices of employers. In addition, the Society also set up schools in several labor camps in the states of New York and Pennsylvania where a wide range of academic subjects were taught. (5)

The Italians, along with other ethnic groups, felt the need to organize their own welfare institutions. The business meetings of the various institutions also met some of the desire for social life. Very early in the Italian migration to the United States, organizations were developed to aid immigrants coming to New York, Boston, New Orleans, St. Louis and elsewhere. Italian groups "were usually connected with a village in the old country, and often had regular social, as well as business, meetings. Members commonly paid an initiation fee of up to $6, then dues of perhaps 25 cents a month. In return they received sickness benefits of $8 to $12 a week, but when a death occurred, a special levy was required. ...apart from aiding the survivors, such a club guaranteed a funeral costing perhaps $50, attended it in a body, and provided a monument." (6)

Those who observed Italian life in the cities of New York and Chicago often described the colorful institution of the 'Fiesta.'

Electric lights were festooned across the streets, arches were put up, flags were draped across the fronts of buildings, concessions were sold for the privilege of having booths on the sidewalk. A special Mass was paid for, and people brought candles or plaques in token of gratitude for favours from their saint, or brought waxen images of bodily parts that had been healed. A procession, led by a priest, centered upon the saint's shrine, carried, then lowered from time to time so that children could kiss the image, and sometimes a blind child would ride for a few yards in the hope of a miracle. Finally, in one version, two children dressed as angels, and carrying armfuls of flowers, were slung on ropes to a position just above the shrine, where they chanted a long prayer. Elsewhere, festivities ended with a firework display. The atmosphere was very like that of the mountain festival in southern Italy....Based on an association related to a village in the old country, and designed to raise funds for it, the ceremonies appear to demonstrate a perfect blending of self-help, a very local patriotism, and the practices of traditional religion. (7)

P.M. Rose, writing in 1922 about the ability of the Italians to organize, came to the following conclusion. "The northern Italian has more initiative, willingness to cooperate, organizing ability. He has also the vices of greater development, he is more sordid, more of a scoffer, more intemperate, and a more expert exploiter than the southernean. The southerner has the vices and virtues of a primitive people, gusty passions of both sex and temper, but vindictive only in certain provinces. There is no greater individualist than he, but he is shrewd, generous, hospitable, tractable, temperate, capable of great devotion, strong of body, although often deformed by his excessive labor." (8) Rose also pointed out that the Italian-Americans consisted of many organizations and opinions but lacked the necessary leadership in the area of bettering their position in the American society. (9)

The Dillingham Commission noted that the new immigrant groups concentrated together. "...the new immigration has been largely a movement of unskilled laboring men who have come, in large part, temporarily, from the less progressive and advanced countries of Europe in response to the call for industrial workers in the eastern and middle western states. They have almost entirely avoided agricultural pursuits, and in cities and industrial communities have congregated together in sections apart from native Americans and older immigrants to such an extent that assimilation has been slow as compared to that of the earlier non-English-speaking races." (10)

Soon after the Italian immigrants came to the United States they started to organize into societies. Charlotte Adams, writing in 1881, pointed out that there were already three Italian societies for mutual assistance - the "Fratellanza Italiana," the "Ticinese," and the "Bersaglieri." When a Fratellanza society member died, his wife received $100; when a wife died, the husband received $50; and a physician was also made available to take care of the sick members of the society. The society staged a ball in the winter and a picnic in the summer. These events were made the occasion for patriotic demonstrations of loyalty to Italy. (11)

In 1905 the Sons of Italy was founded. In 1917 they had 623 lodges in 20 states with a membership of 80,000. In 1915 the Sons of Italy appealed to the New York legislature successfully against a law that claimed that only American citizens could be hired for public works. This law was claimed by labor unions who stopped subway and aqueduct building in New York City and therefore put 18,000 Italians out of work. After the appeal the 18,000 Italians were able to go back to work. In addition, the Sons of Italy urged their members to become American citizens. (12)

In New York City there were developed many Italian benefit societies. One of the most influential was the Italian Chamber of Commerce founded in 1887 and eventually included the majority of Italian businessmen in the city. Its chief objective was to promote, develop and protect the commercial relations between the United States and Italy. (13)

The Italians of New York City organized the Columbus Hospital in 1892 under the supervision of the missionary

Sisters of the Sacred Heart. Columbus Hospital was generally known as an Italian institution; however, of the twenty-one physicians on its staff, not one was an Italian in the first decade of its existence. But, the Sisters of the Sacred Heart were all native Italians and 95% of the patients were Italian. (14)

In 1901 the Italians of New York City founded the Society for the Protection of Italian Immigrants with the purpose of helping the new Italian immigrant make his way in the United States. Working closely with the Society for the Protection of Italian Immigrants was the Italian Benevolent Institute to help the Italian immigrant who found himself in financial trouble or in need of refuge. (15)

Mangano in 1904 pointed out that no bond united the Italian colony in New York City as a whole and that the Italians have a tendency for mutual aid in small groups. "It must be observed, however, that the Italian manifests a strong tendency toward organization with small groups for social ends and for the purpose of mutual aid. There are in Manhattan alone over one hundred and fifty Italian societies of one sort or another." (16)

In New York City the YMCA offered services by meeting immigrants in Italy first and giving them a card directing them to the YMCA authorities in the United States. Due to a lack of money, there was an abortive effort to establish an exclusively Italian branch of the YMCA on the upper East Side. (17)

The Italian immigrant who settled in Cleveland also set about developing mutual benefit organizations. In Cleveland the Italian social organization was divided into roughly four classes: (1) large fraternal organizations having national affiliations; (2) federated societies, a loose but incorporated union of local benefit groups; (3) social clubs, which met mostly at the various settlement houses, many of which were made up of women or permitted mixed membership; and (4) distinctive athletic groups for men and boys. These orders were a big part in the life of the Italian population of Cleveland, stabilizing it and helping to insure the individuals belonging to the various fraternal orders from becoming public charges. It was estimated that more than four-fifths of all the Italian men had membership in one or more of these societies.

Among the small societies in Cleveland was "The Independent Sons of Italy." (different from "Sons of Italy")

This group had less than 100 members but maintained sick benefits and life insurance programs for their members.

The Woodmen of the World and the Oddfellows maintained all-Italian branches in Cleveland which provided full sickness and death benefits. Both of these groups also maintained women's branches.

Before 1917 there were a great many local fraternal societies in Cleveland. Each of these societies had its officers, its own aims and social purposes, along with insurance and other benefit features. Some societies, like the Society of Christopher Columbus, were mutual associations which guaranteed to the deceased member's family $100 towards defraying funeral expenses and an indemnity which was raised by an assessment of $1 on each of the surviving members of the organization. It is clear that an insurance method of this sort is quite precarious. In order to stabilize and standardize indemnities, dues and rates, and to better focus their aims, all the local Italian organizations in Cleveland were united and incorporated in 1917 under the name, "Federated Societies." Each local society represented in the federation did not lose its identity, since the by-laws and rules of the "Federated Societies" had to be ratified by the local organization in order to be enforced. (18)

In the city of Chicago, by 1919, there were 110 private Italian charities and their membership included 90% of the city's Italians. Membership in these organizations were usually from the same Italian province, and often from the same town. Unione Siciliana, with 28 lodges, was the most popular of these organizations. These societies concentrated a great deal of their efforts on sickness and death benefits. The members of the various societies were also required to visit fellow members who were sick if they had no family to take care of them, and to attend funerals of members, at which music was provided by the society. The fees for membership in these societies ranged from 30 to 60 cents per month. Collections were made among Italians for medical treatment if a person did not hold membership in one of the societies. "An unusual spirit of mutual charity is developed among even the poorest Italians of the colonies. Even in times of general poverty it is the exceptional family that refuses a contribution to aid a family in which there is sickness or death." (19)

Settlements, community centers and other agencies working in Chicago Italian districts found that the Italian immigrant was hesitant to take advantage of the services offered by these various agencies. "One reason why the adult Italian manifests this reluctance is because the things offered are distinctly American and have never heretofore been a part of his life experiences. This reluctance should not be interpreted to mean that the adult Italian is opposed to the American shower bath, athletics, or anything else that is distinctly American, but merely that, if he accepts this program, it will be after being educated as to its value." (20)

Professor Humbert S. Nelli points out that "The mutual aid society (societa di mutuo soccorso), although known in Italy, existed almost exclusively among middle classes, and especially among artisans, in urbanized areas of the northern and central parts of the Kingdom." (21) Italian benefit societies in the United States preceded the era of massive immigration from the nations of southern and eastern Europe. (22) Professor Nelli also states that "In order to attract and hold membership, fraternals and mutual aid groups expanded their services from the basic benefit functions to include social ones as well, among them provision for recreational facilities and special annual events, such as picnics, dances, and religious celebrations." (23)

These societies helped the Italian population in the city of Chicago, as well as in other cities, maintain connections with their homeland. "Throughout the 1920s Italian community residents and institutions (press, societies, and church) exhibited an overriding concern for the homeland and its new experiment in government." (24)

In Chicago, there were many clusters of Italian immigrants, each one identified with a particular district in Italy. Professor Vecoli has claimed to identify 17 clusters of Italians living in Chicago from particular districts in the homeland. (25)

The Italian Mutual Aid Society was founded in the city of San Francisco in 1858. It established educational programs for members and hired a physician to take care of those who could not afford to hire one themselves. In 1857, the Society of Italian Union and Fraternity was founded in New York City. In 1864 money was collected from wealthy Italian-Americans to form an evening school for Italian adults. In 1865 the Society of Italian Union raised additional funds to assist widows and orphans of Italian-American soldiers killed during the Civil War and to expand its educational program. By 1881 the Society was paying $100 to widows of deceased members to help defray burial costs, and was providing members with free medical care. As the Italian population in New York City increased, two other mutual aid organizations were founded--Ticinese and the Bersaglieri. As the Italians continued to pour into America, the Society for Italian Immigrants was founded in 1901 to carry on nationwide activities to benefit the Italian immigrant. (26)

The Roman Catholic Church had a minor influence among New York's first Italian-Americans because it offered few organized services. This was due to the Irish dominance of the Catholic Church in the United States. In 1869 there were only 128 Italian priests throughout the United States, according to L'Eco d'Italia. St. Anthony of Padua was established in New York City in 1866, but no Catholic supported associations were set up in New York City before 1880 for the express purpose of aiding the Italian immigrant. "The names of Catholic clergymen were conspicuous for their absence on the governing committees of non-Catholic Italian service organizations. American Protestant laymen and ministers, on the other hand, supported various schools and missions in New York's first 'Little Italy' and performed more effectively in meeting the social problems of these newcomers." A major effort was launched by Protestant missionaries during the early part of the twentieth century to convert the Italian immigrant. (27)

Two professional Italian associations were the Italian Lawyer's Association, founded in 1905, and the Italian Teachers' Association, founded in 1912, which succeeded in introducing Italians into New York City's high school language curriculum. (28)

The most substantial Italian bank in New York City was the Italian Savings Bank, incorporated in 1896. In 1904, this bank had over $1,000,000 on deposit from depositors who were Italian in the great majority. The average sum on deposit was about $170. (29)

In 1912 there were 258 mutual aid societies among Italians in New York City. Over 200 existed in Chicago in 1927. One of the associations formed in New York in 1905 by Dr. Vincent Sellaro, became the Order of the Sons of Italy which had 3,000 lodges in 1957. (30)

The New York Times, on May 31, 1896, reported that out of 105,000 Italians in New York City, at least 25,000 were voting citizens of the United States. Commendatore Louis V. Fugazy was the spiritual head of "Little Italy" and president of approximately 50 mutual aid societies. "...there may be among the Italo-Americans a spirit of independence, seeking a new regime and an up-to-date guidance in social and political affairs peculiar to the prevalent progressive impulse, which suggests a desire to break away from the Old World Conservatism and patriarchal influence of the Commendatore...." The Commendatore's guidance remained in the social and benevolent sphere; he had no political aspirations. When pressed for an opinion, he believed most Italians would follow the lead of their political clubs and would vote Democratic. (31)

The Italian Children's Aid Society was developed in the early 1880s in New York City. Its success was due primarily to aid from prominent New Yorkers as well as the Italian government. It set up school with the objective of helping the Italian children. "Agents were sent among those Italian parents who were wont to employ their children solely for the mercenary purposes of gain, with a selfish disregard for the welfare of their offspring, and as a result of their efforts, in two weeks time alone there were 100 in this class of children gathered into the walls of the Leonard-Street School...." (32)

Also in the 1880s, a home for Italian girls was established near New York City. "The purpose of the institution will be to rear young women for every line of woman's work, to supply trained house servants of a high grade, and also to encourage the development of talent in whatever direction it may be among the inmates. The institution will be conducted by the Sisters of Charity under the patronage of Archbishop Corrigan...." (33)

Italian mutual benefit organizations also strove to protect the Italian immigrant from the padrone (labor boss). The Italo-American Carbonari Association took this responsibility upon themselves. A committee of the Italo-American Carbonari Association of Chicago worked in the major cities and towns, and wherever there were groups of Italian laborers, to try and destroy the padrone system and its Italian banking agencies which cooperate with the padrones. "Respectable Italians are indignant" at the frauds perpetrated by their countrymen, "and are ashamed of the reproach cast upon them of bringing over pauper labor, and the Carbonari branch of this country has already requested the parent society in Italy to bring the matter to the attention of the Italian government." The Chicago and New York Carbonari Association appointed three Italian private detectives in New York City at $75 per month "to ferret out the padrones and the Italian banks that are engaged in the business of trading in human flesh. The names of several padrones in this city were furnished to the Chicago committee, and they will be published in Mazzini Voice, a monthly bulletin of the organization that has a secret circulation among the Carbonari." (34) In order to try to reduce the amount of Italian laborers who became subject to the whims of the padrone, the Carbonari Society tried to have the Italian government pass a law not to allow Italians to emigrate to America without passports and without certificates from the Mayors of their towns in Italy stating that the immigrants have enough money to live on for six months. (35)

John Horace Mariano, in his study of the Italians in 1921, took the view that "the most spontaneous and perhaps the most influential type of grouping that exists in the more thickly populated Italian colonies is the 'social club.' It is inevitable that individuals of the class composing the 'tenement' or 'settlement' type form little groups by themselves. It frequently happens that in a small area of two square blocks there may be four nuclei of groups or cliques that meet together and act for the most part independently of each other." (36)

By 1921, although there were many athletes of Italian extraction in New York City, there was not one Italian athletic club. There were at that time a number of Italian Catholic religious clubs in New York City. An example of one was the Ozanam Association which aimed at the social improvement and social uplift of Italian Americans with an attempt to keep up religious practices. Of the 600,000 Italians in New York City, the Roman Catholic Church, by its own figures, was able to claim only 180,135 members. This is a very significant figure when, during that period of time only, 3% of the Italians living in Italy were classified as Protestant. (37)

By the early 1920s the Italians of New York City had formed many mutual benefit groups such as social clubs, religious clubs, benevolent associations, civic organizations, social welfare clubs, The Italian League for Social Service, The Italian Educational League which worked for the betterment of Italian pupils, the Italian Welfare League, College Italian Clubs called 'Italian Circolo' (Italian word for club), Italian Medical Society, Italian Teachers' Association, The Italian Lawyers' Association, and The Italian National Club where people of Italian ancestry could meet and get to know one another. (38)

Enrico C. Sartorio, writing in 1918, observed that not all Italian organizations were a good thing. He pointed out that various local clubs caused Italian boys and girls to stay out, away from home, almost every evening. "The club-trained Italian boys and girls are easily recognized by the ease with which they get married and divorced, by their willingness to stay and take care of their home after they are married, by their almost insane desire to be necessarily out for 'a good time,' and by their lack of respect for their old people. This would not be the case if clubs were so organized as to include both the young people and their parents, keeping thus the whole family together, on the same social plane." (39)

In the city of Philadelphia an Italo-America League was formed in 1891 for the purpose "That Italians shall not be a foreign horde, but become American citizens...for which an important organization to be known as the Italo-American League is to be formed in this city." Among the 20,000 Italians in Philadelphia in 1891, there existed over 20 secret societies which were subject to jealousies. The Italo-American League movement was seen as a forerunner of similar movements to be established in other urban areas. A.W. Horton, main organizer of the League, stated that "...through the medium of the Italo-American League the enactment of laws looking toward the suppression of low and degrading avocations carried on by Italians, such as organ-grinding; to establish a bureau and to encourage the full exercise of the rights of American citizenship without...influencing the political opinions of the members...." Horton also stated that the League will act on behalf of the Italian-Americans. (40)

During the 1920s Italian-Americans were very interested in Mussolini's government in Italy. Most American Italians greeted the Mussolini government with enthusiasm during the 1920s.

In 1935 "The Nation" published articles in which the Casa Italiana (the Italian cultural center located at Columbia University) was accused of being dominated by Fascists and disseminating Fascist propaganda. Nicholas Murray Butler, the President of Columbia University, denied these accusations, but the intensity of the charges caused him to ask the Casa Italiana to concentrate their interests on non-political affairs.

When many people think of Italian organizations they mistakenly think of the Mafia. "Perplexing is the fact that the Mafia as a formal organization does not exist. There are no Mafia headquarters, no Mafia offices. The Mafia has no written statutes, no lists of members, no fixed rules. The question of who becomes a Mafia leader is an obscure matter of family prestige, influenced by personality and force, and never the result of balloting. The Mafia can be defined as a haphazard collection of men and groups, each working independently in local situations by cooperating with each other to control its interests in the economic life of an area." (41)

The Italian immigrant press played an important part in the Italian community as other immigrant presses played in various immigrant communities. The Italian immigrant press saw itself as a bridge between the 'homeland' and America. They helped make the transition of the immigrant easier and helped him to feel a part of things by enabling him to obtain information about various events in Italy and the United States before his ability to understand English well enough enabled him to read the American newspapers. The Italian immigrant press told the new immigrant about a variety of things - news of Italy, news of the Italo-American community, news of education, news of politics, information about American customs and practices and other topics of special interest to the Italian population.

During the 1870s, L'Eco d'Italia became very influential within the Italian community. In 1876 the paper endorsed Ulysses S. Grant for re-election to the Presidency. The paper reported on the growing influence of the Italians in American politics. A section of L'Eco d'Italia was devoted to "Italian Art in America." This feature spoke of the many contributions of Italian artists in the United States.

By the end of the first decade of the 20th century there were six Italian daily newspapers in New York City with a circulation varying between 10,000 and 30,000 per day. Half of those newspapers had a greater circulation outside of the city and all maintained special agents to search for subscribers in labor camps, small towns and mining areas. The earliest Italo-American newspapers were mainly translations from the American press. Eventually, as the quality of the Italian press improved in New York City, it still did not maintain a cable service from Italy. "While a great part of the advertising of the Italian newspapers comes from steamship companies, professional men, importers and merchants, there is still too large a portion from fake doctors, real estate swindlers, and alleged brokers who sell to the immigrant the stock of companies that do not exist. However, there are two Italian dailies that enjoy the distinction of having refused money offered for political support at the last municipal election, and of having helped the Fusion cause without recompense--a startling reform in Italian journalism. It is to be hoped that in the future the Italian press may not confine its benevolent activities to the providing of the city with monuments to Italian worthies, but that it will attempt to instruct the Italian masses with regard to their duties in their new environment. (42)

In 1918, Enrico Sartorio also had criticism of the Italian press in America. He emphasized that articles printed about America in Italian-American newspapers "are written by people who have lived all their lives among Italians and, being prejudiced through their lack of understanding of the new country in which they live, are ready to misrepresent it; or they are written by unscrupulous men who play upon popular feeling and endeavor to get into the good graces of the subscribers by exalting everything Italiano and decrying everything American." Sartorio also stressed the fact that criticisms of American life were often offered by writers unfamiliar with the culture of America. (43)

According to Antonio Mangano, writing in 1919, the two chief Italian newspapers were Il Progresso Italiano and Il Carrocio of New York. Il Progresso Italiano was the most prominent newspaper of Italian immigrants. It dealt with collecting funds for such things as the erection of monuments to honor worthy Italians and to send aid to Italy when disaster occurs. It is still being published. Il Carrocio of New York dealt with literature, politics and science and had patriotic and ethical information. Another Italian newspaper of the time, Il Cittadino, established by Protestant ministers and published in Chicago and New York, was devoted to the reformation of Italian life and the Italian press. Mangano went on to explain that excluding these three newspapers, the Italian press "...does not have a sufficiently high ideal of its mission. It occupies itself too much with slander and in many cases expresses sentiments that are un-American. It lacks high ethical standards. It is generally under the control of one or the other of the two political parties, and its utterances are biased because of that relationship." (44)

In spite of its many faults, the Italian language newspapers in the United States played an important role in helping the Italian immigrant adjust to his new country. For the poorly educated Southern Italian immigrant, the newspapers helped him to receive valuable information about his new homeland and helped him still retain a sense of identity with Italy. The newspapers were written simply with the type of prose that a poorly educated immigrant could understand and helped to give the new immigrant a sense of belonging. There is very little doubt that the Italian language press was a very important benefit organization to the Italian immigrant.

During the latter part of the 1960s a new development in Italian organizations took place. In part because of the Negro movement of the 1960s, other ethnic groups in America have become more aware of their own self-identity. The Italian-American also became more vocal in establishing his own group solidarity.

In March, 1966, the American Italian Anti-Defamation League, composed of over 7,000 members, was founded. The first president of the organization was New York City Council Judge Ross J. DiLorenzo. The judge claimed that his organization was designed to prevent the media from using such terms as "Mafia" and employing the "...stereotype criminal in movies...always dark-complexioned, and his last name always ends in a vowel. Judge DiLorenzo also objected to the use of the term "Mafia" for it connoted that organized crime is the monopoly of the Italians when such is not the case. The National Chairman of this organization was Frank Sinatra. (45) In March, 1968, the American Italian Anti-Defamation League changed its name to Americans of Italian Descent. (46)

The Americans of Italian Descent adopted a new program designed to stress "constructive contributions of Italian-Americans"; to help the Italo-American community improve itself; to provide youth with legal counsel, job opportunities; to cooperate with higher education; to raise money for hospitals and to work for better relations with all. (47)

In June, 1970, Italian Americans picketed the F.B.I. Building in New York City for discrimination against Italians. The Italian Americans were then brought before the New York State Supreme Court for disruption of the peace. The first of these picketings was led by Colombo to protest the arrest of his son Joseph Colombo Jr. on April 30, 1970. (48) Colombo, reputed head of one of the New York Mafia's six families, had been cited as the organizer behind the protests at the F.B.I. headquarters. Law enforcement agents felt that the average protester thought he had a legitimate complaint, but they were really just pawns of Colombo's button-men. The New York Times pointed out, "...the alleged defamation of Italians by the F.B.I. is something many people - not just those of Italian lineage - believe is a problem." (49)

Another organization, the Italian-American Civil Rights League, was formed in 1970. By April, 1971 it claimed a membership of 45,000 within 19 states. "The League says the F.B.I., the Federal Organized Crime Strike Force, United States Attorney General and President Nixon are embarked upon a vindictive campaign against Italian-Americans in general and the League in particular." Within the Italian-American Civil Rights League, middle-age and middle-class persons predominate, although there are many enthusiastic young among its leadership. The League endorsed Mario Biaggi (Dem-Bronx), community control and school reform (abolition of Board of Examiners in New York City), and patriotism. Its first president was Natale Marcone and its first vice-president was Anthony Colombo. The League called Joe Colombo its founder and the one who established the atmosphere of league action. The purpose of the Italian-American Rights League is to fight discrimination against Italians with special emphasis on the association of Italians with crime. (50) On June 28, 1971 Anthony Colombo was wounded by a Negro gunman at the Italian American Civil Rights Rally at Columbus Circle in New York City. At present most Italian groups are taking a greater interest in combatting anti-Italian discrimination, especially in the area of economic discrimination.

As one can see, mutual benefit organizations have played an important part in the adjustment and assimilation of the Italian immigrant to the United States.

Source Notes

(1) Humbert S. Nelli, "Ethnic Group Assimilation: The Italian Experience," Cities in American History, ed. Kenneth T. Jackson and Stanley K. Schultz (New York: Alfred A. Knopf, 1972), p. 203.

(2) Nathan Glazer and Daniel P. Moynihan, Beyond the Melting Pot (Cambridge, Mass.: M.I.T. Press), p. 186.

(3) Alberto Periconi, "The Italians in the United States," Forum, LXV (January, 1911), p. 24.

(4) Luciano J. Iorizzo and Salvadore Mondello, The Italian American (New York: Twayne Publishers, Inc., 1971), pp. 100-101.

(5) Ibid., pp. 102-103.

(6) Philip Taylor, The Distant Magnet: European Emigration to the U.S.A. (New York: Harper & Row Publishers, 1971), pp. 214-215.

(7) Ibid., p. 237.

(8) Phillip M. Rose, The Italians in America (New York: George H. Doran Co., 1922), p. 37.

(9) Ibid., p. 90.

(10) Reports of the Immigration Commission, 1907-1910. 41 vols. Vol. I, Senate Documents of 61st Congress, 3d Session (Washington, D.C.: Government Printing Office, 1911), p. 14.

(11) Charlotte Adams, "Italian Life in New York," Harper's Magazine, LXII (April, 1881), p. 678.

(12) Antonio Manzano, Sons of Italy: A Social and Religious Study of the Italians in America (New York: Missionary Education Movement of the United States and Canada, 1919), p. 129.

(13) Antonio Manzano, "The Associated Life of the Italians in New York City," Charities, XII (May 7, 1904), p. 478.

(14) Ibid.

(15) Ibid., pp. 478-479.

(16) Ibid., p. 479.

(17) Manzano, Sons of Italy, p. 138.

(18) Charles W. Coulter, The Italians of Cleveland
(Cleveland: Americanization Committee, 1919), pp.
34-36.

(19) Frank Orman Beck, The Italian in Chicago (Chicago:
Chicago Department of Public Welfare Bulletin,
1919), pp. 22-23.

(20) Ibid., p. 24.

(21) Humbert S. Nelli, The Italians in Chicago, 1880-1930
(New York: Oxford University Press, 1970), p.
170.

(22) Ibid., p. 171.

(23) Ibid., p. 176.

(24) Ibid., p. 239.

(25) Rudolph J. Vecoli, "Contadini in Chicago," Journal of
American History, LI (1964-65), 408.

(26) Iorizzo and Mondello, op. cit., pp. 27-28.

(27) Ibid., pp. 28-29.

(28) Ibid., p. 94.

(29) Manzano, "The Associated Life of Italians in New York
City," p. 482.

(30) Iorizzo and Mondello, op. cit., p. 95.

(31) New York Times, May 31, 1896, p. 32.

(32) New York Times, January 16, 1882, p. 4.

(33) New York Times, February 25, 1886, p. 3.

(34) New York Times, February 1, 1888, p. 2.

(35) New York Times, February 7, 1888, p. 8.

(36) John Horace Mariano, The Italian Contribution to Ameri-
      can Democracy. With an Introduction by F.H.
      LaGuardia (Boston: The Christopher Publishing
      House, 1921), p. 140.

(37) Ibid., pp. 144-148.

(38) Ibid., pp. 140-181.

(39) Enrico C. Sartorio, Social and Religious Life of Italians
      in America (Boston: The Christopher Publishing
      House, 1918), p. 72.

(40) New York Times, May 4, 1891, p. 1.

(41) Andre F. Rolle, The Immigrant Upraised (Norman:
      University of Oklahoma Press, 1968), p. 106.

(42) Periconi, op. cit., p. 25.

(43) Sartorio, op. cit., p. 42.

(44) Manzano, Sons of Italy, p. 126.

(45) New York Times, April 14, 1967, p. 23.

(46) New York Times, March 26, 1968, p. 42.

(47) New York Times, April 3, 1968, p. 49.

(48) New York Times, June 6, 1970, p. 19.

(49) New York Times, June 9, 1970, p. 1.

(50) New York Times, April 4, 1971, p. 64.

Chapter III

CRIME AND ECONOMIC DEVELOPMENT OF
THE ITALIAN-AMERICAN

The problem of urban lawlessness and crime was deeply rooted in that of the slums. Vile places like "Misery Row," "Poverty Lane" and "Murderers' Alley" were both continuous recruiting grounds for juvenile delinquents and hiding places for criminal bands. Lacking normal outlets for play, the tenement waifs naturally drifted into gangs in which what might have been a laudable spirit of group loyalty was twisted into an ambition to emulate the lawless exploits of their elders. Beginning as beggars, sneak thieves and pickpockets, they graduated all too quickly into the ranks of shoplifters, robbers and thugs. The foreign origin of many of the slum dwellers made this transition all the easier because of prior unfamiliarity with American traditions and laws. In particular the Irish and Italians contributed more than their proportionate share of the country's prison population, though it was the American-born immigrant child, lacking proper parental guidance, and wholesome surroundings, who turned most readily to underworld life. (1)

Probably no group has been more villified over the problem of crime than the Italian-American. In order to achieve a greater understanding of the nature of crime among the Italian-Americans it is necessary to explore this problem. Before proceeding one should keep in mind the connection between economics and crime among the Italian-Americans.

Italians, suffering from the effects of a depression and discrimination, made up a large proportion of New York City's slum population in the 1870s. Their living conditions were hurt by overcrowding and many living in these slums were the victims of malaria. Secchi de Casali, writing in L'Eco d'Italia, in 1880, "noted with trepidation the rising numbers of South Italian poor entering the city." The writer was of the opinion that the influx of South Italians could cause a resurgence of prejudice against all Italians living in New York City, and that Italians from Southern Italy would gain nothing by residing in the city's crowded and filthy slums. (2)

According to an observer writing in 1915, the cause of Italian increase in crime upon arrival in the United States was: "Apart from the lure and demoralizing effect of life on city streets, the real reason is loss of parental control. The parent speaks one language, the child another. The child put to work at fourteen feels he is grown-up, he is earning money, and has a right to his own way." (3)

It appears that the crimes of the Italian immigrant was usually against the person as opposed to property. (4) The New York Times on March 5, 1882 reported: Italian peasants, "low as they are, are not often found in our prisons for crimes of theft and robbery. They seem to be on the whole an honest class, but they are continually brought before the courts for fighting, violence, and attempts at murder--crimes which arise from the crowded way in which they live and the jealousies and quarrels that would naturally arise from such a promiscuous mode of life." (5) In 1884, the Times pointed out that "The case of Italian brigandage in Second Avenue seems to have startled timid people....The Italians who come to this country with a hereditary respect for brigandage, and find that the men who are most talked of here are the Jesse Jameses of the West and the Jay Goulds of the East, naturally think that there is a fine field in America for genuine Italian brigandage." (6)

Enrico Sartorio, an Italian immigrant who lectured at the Cambridge Episcopal Theological School, stated in 1918 that "Many so-called crimes among Italians are not crimes at all from a certain viewpoint and many mistakes are made through the enforcement in the case of Italians of a law that was drawn up for Anglo-Saxons. The state of political administration which existed in Italy, and especially the Southern part, only a short time ago, practically compelled a man to take the law into his own hands in order to safeguard his interests, his family and his life. We in America have something of an illustration of this in the Western life of the last generation. When an Italian kills a man, it is generally ascribed to the spirit of vendetta....The tribal or clanish spirit is very strong among Italians of a certain type and what you regard as a criminal tendency may be considered, if you study the traditions of these people, as a manifestation of chivalry. Think of the feuds of the Kentucky mountains between individuals of the purest English stock!" (7) Sartorio, also pointed out that

Sicilians possess "an inborn distrust and hatred of authority" because of centuries of misgovernment and the Bourbon police system and they are reluctant to put private differences before government officials, because their cost of honor called "omerta" (manliness) mandates that these differences be settled privately. (8) Leonard Covello showed the enormous amount of loyalty to one's family when he said: "It is impossible to imagine the 'contadino' (peasant) in South Italy contributing to the Red Cross." (9) An example of this is that in South Italy morality is limited to the family. An old woman saw a boy steal fruit from a tree and ignores this. She then saw him stealing a second time and severely reproached him for this. It seems that in the first instance, he was stealing from a stranger but in the second instance he was stealing from someone who was part of his family. (11)

Glazer and Moynihan stated that this moral code remained among the Italian immigrants who came to America. "One should not trust strangers, and may advance one's interest at the cost of strangers. Also, one does not interfere in strangers' business. One therefore tolerates the breaking of law by others." (11)

Robert Foerster, in 1919, claimed that the American attitude towards the Italian is in part due to his record of crime. "Elemental natures seem to be at work. Abducting, kidnapping, rape, stand forth, and the newspapers glory in the details. The knife is used by men in their senses, by sober men; and a startling record of homicides or of attempted homicides appears. It is the Old World way. That the victims are themselves Italians, and that the roots of the dispute often lie in the past or in a misadventure of love, is insufficiently realized." (12)

One of the strongest examples of Italian crime was the "Black Hand." A wealthy man receives a message demanding a sum of money of the "Black Hand." If the message is not received the person meets his death by knife or bomb. During the first seven months of 1913 there were sixty Italian murders in New York City. The perpetrators of these crimes were most likely members of the 'Camorra' or 'Mafia.' "Although few attacks have been made upon others than Italians and most have been in New York, yet the terrorization has affected a larger circle. Since no 'Mano Nera' (Black Hand) exists in Italy, we may say that the whole development has been conditioned by imported criminals or by criminals bred in the American environment-assimilated, if you will, to bad elements rather than to good--and by the presence of a large community of aliens. The constant unwillingness of the Italians to act as witnesses in the courts has made the suppression of Black Hand crime, as of Italian crime, generally all the more difficult." (13)

In 1893, the New York Times contended that the illiterate peasants of Southern Italy "...having had no feeling, save contempt and hatred for the courts of their native land, do not import with them any disposition to respect the processes of civil tribunals in this country. Taught to seek redress with stiletto or blunderbuss at home, they cannot be easily educated to outgrow that inclination, especially where they continue to herd together, to speak only their native patois, and to nurture their inherited prejudices and traditions." (14)

It has been observed that some Italians brought to the United States some less attractive features of life in Southern Italy and centuries-old vendettas were fought in the streets of America's largest cities. In 1913, it was commented on by one critic that United States immigration legislation made it easy for Italian criminals to enter the country. Also ineffective extradition procedures on the part of the United States devastated the Italian government's efforts to secure those criminals who had escaped the observance of the Italian emigration authorities. Many reformers believed that police protection would be improved if more Italians were brought into the New York City police force. In 1908 the city only had 40 Italian policemen. As crime increased in "Little Italies" many Americans blamed this on the low moral and educational levels of the South Italian who permitted the machinations of an enormous criminal conspiracy in the United States, as it permitted the practices of the "Mafia" in Italy. (15)

An article in Forum in 1901 stated that Italy was among the leaders in homicides, but the writer claimed that homicides in Italy were declining in part "because emigration is generally undertaken by men, and, for the most part, youths, who yield the largest proportion of homicides." (16)

In 1909, Arthur Woods, former deputy police commissioner in New York City, stated that the 'Black Handers' "are men who have left criminal records behind them in Italy....In New York it has been found in almost every case that a man arrested for a Black Hand crime has been convicted of crime in Italy. They settle down in communities of wage-earning Italians wherever they can find them and then proceed to prey upon them. So far, then, from being criminals themselves the

vast majority of the Italian immigrants here are in need of
defense against the criminals. The Black Handers are para-
sites, fattening off the main body of their fellow-country-
men. They are Italian criminals who prefer to make their
living by extortion rather than by the sweat of their faces.
From this it will readily be seen that the Black Hand is not a
cohesive, comprehensive society, working with mysterious
signs and passwords. Given a number of Italians with money,
and two or three ex-convicts, you have all the elements necessary for a first-rate Black Hand campaign." (17) The Black
Handers were known to exploit the poor, illiterate laborer. In
1911 another observer stated that: "These predal opportunists
flatter him in magnificent articles published in weekly newspapers and magazines that are born and die in the Italian
quarters with wonderful rapidity; they get money for sub-
scriptions to and advertisements in newspapers that are never
published at all; they take his part in foolish quarrels with
equally vain competitors for the presidency of a society...and,
after all other expedients have been employed, they demand
money with threatening letters, kidnap his children, or put a
stick of dynamite in his cellar." (18)

Americans react with a great degree of emotional outbreak towards Italian crime. Between 1890 and 1920 the word
'Mafia' and tales of Italian crime were predominant in American
newspapers. Some Italian community leaders responded by
denying the existence of the Mafia and some Italian-language
newspapers shortly after 1900 began using the term 'Black
Hand' to identify criminal activities that occurred within the
Italian community. Therefore, the term 'Black Hand' was used
during the first two decades of the twentieth century. The
crimes committed by the 'Black Hand' were limited almost
entirely to the Sicilian and southern-Italian neighborhoods.
Black Hand activities took a decided turn downward in the
1920s, for a number of reasons. First, the number of pliable
victims decreased after immigration was terminated during
World War I and by subsequent restrictive legislation of the
1920s. Second, the federal government began enforcing laws
which prohibited using the mails for the purpose of defraud,
thus forcing Black Hand notes to be delivered personally.
Neighborhood hoodlums, wanting to remain anonymous, found
this activity to be too much of a risk. While these factors
were limiting opportunities for criminal activity within the
Italian quarter, a new field of criminal endeavor had developed
within the wider American community. Before January 16,
1920, when the Volstead Act which prohibited the manufacturing and sale of alcoholic beverages in the United States went
into effect, the majority of Italian lawbreakers worked within

the Italian colony. The drinking habits of the American public did not conform to the new prohibition regulations, and law-breakers saw tremendous opportunities for huge profits. Former Black Handers, unemployed immigrants, and young gang members turned their eyes to the illegal but lucrative liquor business, which they eventually controlled in New York, Chicago, and other large cities. The restriction of immigration and Prohibition brought the Black Hand era to an end and acquainted many Italian immigrants with the central core of American gangsterism. (19)

With the passage of the Volstead Act, bootlegging produced the main source of income for gangs which were so prominent in the large cities of America. In 1920 'Scarface' Al Capone began his hoodlum empire in Chicago. This empire controlled alcohol, gambling, prostitution and drugs in the Chicago area. Capone was a New York City hoodlum from the Five Points Gang who, by 1927, was operating a $60,000,000 business and had a personal army of approximately one thousand men who killed rival bootleggers who attempted to break into Capone's 'territory.' In 1926 and 1927 there were 130 gangland killings in Cook County, Illinois and not one of the murderers was apprehended. Capone drove the streets of Chicago in an armor-plated automobile worth thirty thousand dollars, escorted by a bevy of scout cars, and he went to the theatre surrounded by a flock of bodyguards. Once when Capone was brought in by the police for interrogation, one hundred of his gangsters beseiged the Detective Bureau. (20)

Italian underworld activities, although most often linked to Chicago in the 1920s and 1930s, also had its hand in the East as shown by this excerpt from the New York Times concerning the murder of two men in New Jersey. "The bodies of two men trussed with cord and weighted sash weights were found this afternoon several miles apart floating in waters adjacent to Newark." The newspaper also pointed out that the police were working on the theory that these men (Sam Monaco of East Orange, N.J., and his partner Luigi Russo of Newark, N.J.) were killed in a gang war over the sale of alcohol or beer. (21)

Salvatore Maranzano, who was stabbed and gunned down on September 10, 1931, was a New York businessman and was involved in both bootlegging and a nationwide ring of alien smugglers. The New York Times reported that: "A murder yesterday afternoon in a midtown New York office building sent a dozen detectives hurrying out of town on secret missions last night, and it is said to have furnished the police and District Attorney's Office with the startling disclosures regarding the operations of a nationwide ring of alien smugglers. The existence of such a ring has long been known to the Federal authorities. It is estimated that more than 8,000 aliens have been smuggled into the United States by this means in recent years, and earlier this week it was revealed nineteen arrests had been made here. Only a few weeks ago the government began an investigation, centering its activity on the Chicago territory of Al Capone. And the fact that yesterday's murder has been linked with Chicago gunmen is therefore regarded as significant." (22)

One of the most notorious incidents of crime involving the Italians was the "St. Valentine's Day Massacre" of 1929. In this massacre seven Chicago gangsters were killed by a firing squad of rival gangsters. The gangsters killed be- / longed to the George (Bugs) Maran-Dean O'Banion, North Side Gang. "The seven gang warriors were trapped in a beer distributers' rendezvous at 2122 North Clark Street, lined up against the wall by four men, two of whom were in police uniforms, and executed with the precision of a firing squad." These killings grew out of a gang war disputing the control of the illegal liquor traffic. (23)

The Mafia, as a formal organization, does not exist. There are no official headquarters, laws, members or a set of rules. The determination of who becomes a Mafia leader is a matter of family prestige, personality and force. There is never an election to make this determination. "The Mafia can be defined as a haphazard collection of men and groups, each working independently in local situations but cooperating with each other to control its interests in the economic life of an area." (24)

The Mafia began by Sicilians in reaction against the incursions of French, Spanish and Austrians into Sicily before the Italian Peninsula achieved independence. The Mafia recruited people with the purpose of protecting their homes, families and themselves from the foreigners who held authority over them. "They established their own judicial system, hired their own police (the mafiosi), and collected taxes from those who wished protection from the foreigners. Many thus "came to find a swifter and more equitable form of justice in the local Mafia societies than what the so-called legitimate governments offered." (25)

Further reasons for the growth of the Mafia in 19th century Italy was due to the abuses of the feudal system and

Spanish misrule. "By then, the Mafia had become an association of loosely organized, small criminal bands (cosche) which specialized in cattle rustling, extortion, and kidnapping....In short, in response to foreign oppression, the Mafia became in reality a way of life for Sicilians living mainly in the western and rural parts of the Island." A secret society similar to the Mafia was formed in Naples around 1820. Known as the Camorra, its purpose was that "of giving protection to its members, many of whom were recently released political prisoners." Though this group helped Garibaldi against the Austrians, its criminal elements soon obtained control of the organization. (26)

With the immigration of a large number of Italians from Sicily to America, the loosely organized Mafia and Camorra also moved elements of their organization to where their fellow Italians settled.

Many Italians in the United States achieved enormous financial reward from organized crime. "At a time when 'American' Italians (those born or raised in the United States) were arriving at maturity only to find economic advancement made difficult - but not impossible - by inadequate education, 'undesirable' social and ethnic backgrounds, and lack of political connections, a new field of endeavor appeared, requiring as qualifications only ambition, ruthlessness and loyalty." (27)

Early in prohibition, Johnny Torrio of Chicago concluded that bootlegging meant profits. He hired Al Capone as his lieutenant. By the mid 1920s Capone controlled the suburb of Cicero. Violence, gang wars, murder, crime and corruption ruled in Chicago. Italians possessing strong economic and political influence in the windy city made spectacular and notorious inroads into the mainstream of Chicago's life during the 1920s. (28) Italians like Capone, Torrio, Drucci, the Aiellos, the Gennas and other Sicilians became millionaires during the prohibition years. Estimates of Capone's syndicate's gross annual income were from $100,000,000 to over $300,000,000 by the late 1920s. The prohibition era proved to be a Golden Age for America's gangsters and especially for the second generation Southern Italians who were able to amass a tremendous amount of wealth and power. (29)

Ironically, to many of the Italians living in Chicago, Al Capone appeared to be a modern day Robin Hood. In the city of Chicago, and its suburb of Cicero, Capone's benevolence, like the criminal organization that he headed (and that provided the cash for his welfare activities), reached beyond his fellow 'Southerners.' The 'Big Fellow' opened his wallet and his 'syndicate' to anyone, regardless of race, creed, or color. Novelist Mary Borden, who in 1930 visited her native Chicago after an absence of twelve years, described Capone as 'an ambidextrous giant, who kills with one hand and feeds with the other.'" (30)

Daniel Bell, in his book, The End of Ideology, noted that the Senate Crime Committee failed in its attempt to prove with real evidence, the existence of a crime syndicate known as the Mafia. He attributed this failure to a lack of understanding of "three of the more relevant sociological facts about institutionalized crime in its relation to the political life of large urban communities in America, namely: 1) the rise of the American-Italian community, as part of the inevitable process of ethnic succession, to positions of importance in politics, a process that has been occurring independently but also simultaneously in most cities with large Italian constituencies - New York, Chicago, Kansas City, Los Angeles; 2) the fact that there are individual Italians who play prominent, often leading roles today in gambling and the mobs; and 3) the fact that Italian gamblers and mobsters often possessed 'status' within the Italian community itself and a 'pull' in city politics."

Bell stated that the Italians did not achieve wealth or political power through the same routes as did earlier immigrant groups. Their way was much harder, and came later than for the others. Italians "...found the more obvious big city paths from rags to riches preempted." As Jacob Riis said, "...the Italian comes in at the bottom and stays there." Referring to the monopoly that the Irish have over the Italian Catholics regarding their numbers in the hierarchy of the Church, Bell states that this condition "...is a factor related to the politics of the American Church; but the condition is also possible because there is not significant or sufficient wealth among Italian Americans to force some parity." Therefore, the Italian found himself in a precarious position. "Excluded from the political ladder - in the early thirties there were almost no Italians on the city payroll in top jobs, nor in books of the period can one find discussion of Italian political leaders - and finding few routes open to wealth, some turned to illicit ways. In the children's court statistics of the 1930s, the largest group of delinquents were the Italian; nor were there any Italian communal or social agencies to cope with these problems. Yet it was, oddly enough, the quondam racketeer, seeking to become respectable, who provided one of the major supports for the drive to win a political voice for

Italians in the power structure of the urban political machines."

The rise of Italian political power was connected with the new methods employed by the urban political machines to raise money. One of these methods was to 'tax' those city workers who fought for higher wages from the city. Another was to tax gamblers, and a third was from the recently, though perhaps illegally earned, Italian money. Such contributions to the machine facilitated entrance into politics.

Frank Costello originally made money from bootlegging. Huey Long offered him the opportunity to set up slot machines in Louisiana. Striking it rich, he later invested in real estate and the famous Copacabana Night Club. His entrance into politics stemmed from his rendering of financial aid to the floundering Tammany machine of post LaGuardia days. "The Italian community in New York has for years nursed a grievance against the Irish and, to a lesser extent, the Jewish political groups for monopolizing political power. They complained about the lack of judicial jobs, the small number - usually one - of Italian congressmen, the lack of representation of the state tickets....Italian immigrants, largely poor peasants from southern Italy and Sicily, lacked the mercantile experience of the Jews and the political experience gained in the seventy-five year history of Irish immigration."

During the Prohibition era the Italians made several inroads into politics through the Tammany machine. Al Marinelli, backed by Lucky Luciano of underworld and drug-peddling fame, ran for district leader of the West Side. In 1932 he was the lone Italian in Tammany. Costello had previously established communication with Jimmy Hines, a powerful West Side Tammany man.

In 1937, Thomas Dewey accused Marinelli of affiliation with gangsters and he was dismissed from his post as county clerk by Governor Herbert Lehman of New York. District Attorney Dewey also engineered Hines' and Luciano's convictions, and much of Italian funding of Tammany was redirected through Costello. Within a few years, a number of Italian judges were appointed due to the proper connections with some Irish and Jewish politicos and a large bulk of Italian leaders in Tammany.

Mayor Fiorello LaGuardia of New York City was well aware of where the source of many of his campaign funds lay. However, he later turned against fellow Italians, notably

Costello, who reached his high point in 1942. During this period other Italian political leaders were becoming prominent. Generoso Pope, who purchased the two largest Italian-language dailies (which were later merged into one) and a radio station, became a very important political figure because of an almost complete monopoly of the channels of communication to the Italian-speaking population of New York City. Because of the activities of Generoso Pope and Frank Costello, the Italians became a powerful political influence in New York City. It is interesting to note that "...the motive for establishing Italian political prestige in New York was generous rather than scheming for personal advantage. For Costello it was largely a case of ethnic pride. As in earlier American eras, organized illegality became a stepladder of social ascent."

Bell pointed out that "The early Italian gangsters were hoodlums - rough, unlettered and young (Al Capone was only twenty-nine at the height of his power). Those who survived learned to adapt. By now [Bell is referring to the 1950s] they are men of middle age or older. They learned to dress conservatively. Their homes are in respectable suburbs. They sent their children to good schools and sought to avoid publicity. Costello even went to a psychiatrist in his efforts to overcome a painful feeling of inferiority in the world of manners."

Bell also concluded that "Ironically, the social development which made possible the rise of political influence sounds, too, the knell of the rough Italian gangster. For it is the growing number of Italians with professional training and legitimate business success that both prompts and permits the Italian group to wield increasing political influence; and increasingly it is the professionals and businessmen who provide models for Italian youth today....Ironically, the headlines and exposes of 'crime' of the Italian 'gangsters' came years after the fact." (31)

The Italian community received bad publicity dealing with crime in the case of Mayor Hugh Addonizio of Newark, New Jersey. Mayor Addonizio ran for re-election despite the fact that he was under indictment by the Federal government for extortion and income tax evasion. He, along with fourteen others, was charged with extorting $253,000 from a construction company doing business with the city of Newark while he was mayor. (32) Ultimately, Addonizio lost a special mayoralty election to Kenneth Gibson. Addonizio was ultimately found guilty by a Federal jury on 64 counts, one of conspiracy and 63 of extortion. (33)

Over the years the Italians have been pictured as a group of people who commit a very high percentage of the crime in the United States. This has been a gross exaggeration and has led to a malignment of a group of people who do not deserve it. In the remainder of this chapter evidence will be presented that will illustrate that the reports of Italian crime that have circulated over the years have been exaggerated. The Italians have not had the lowest proportion of crime in any ethnic group in this country, but the appearance of them having close to the highest, if not the highest, has been wrong.

By the turn of the twentieth century, many Americans were troubled by the influx of immigration into the United States. They viewed the new wave of immigrants as being inferior to the old wave of immigrants. This growth of nativism (34) on the part of many Americans led to the Congress forming the Immigration Commission, 1907-1910 (better known as the Dillingham Commission), to study the effects of the immigrant on American society. From reading the commission reports it appears clear that it constantly sought to prove the detrimental effects of the new immigration on American society.

The Commission's greatest fallacy lay in the techniques it employed as it geared its scientific investigation towards proving preconceived conclusions - namely that the new immigration, differing from the older immigration in various ways, was decidedly inferior. Not seeking to prove the difference between immigrant waves, or even present a rational comparison, the Commission also omitted to study the immigrant groups over a sufficient period of time; they neglected to use valuable data on that subject that was accessible from various government bureaus; and they offered conclusions predicated on little evidence. (35)

However, even with the Commission's biases, their findings about the Italian immigrant does not show him in a completely negative light.

The Dillingham Commission in its conclusions found that from available statistics it did not appear that the criminality among the foreign-born caused an increase in the amount of criminal activity in proportion to the total population. (36)

The Immigration Commission found that in the areas of blackmail and extortion, the total crimes of Italians was in excess of that of any other race and nationality. The Commission also found that the Italians also led the other races and nationalities in having the highest percentage of abduction, kidnapping, homicide and were among the leaders in the crimes of larceny, robbery, burglary and rape. (37)

The Immigration Commission also stated that: "The Italians have the highest percentages of the aggregate offenses of personal violence shown by the data from the New York City Magistrates' Courts, the New York Court of General Sessions, the County and Supreme Courts of New York State, and the penal institutions of Massachusetts. The Chicago police records alone show a different condition; in them the Italian percentage is exceeded by those of the Lithuanians and Slavonians, neither of which nationalities appears as a separate group....Certain specific crimes in personal violence also belong distinctively to Italian criminality. Abduction and kidnapping in the figures from the New York City Magistrates' Courts and the County and Supreme Courts of New York State form a larger percentage of the crimes of Italians than of those of any other group of offenders. In the Chicago figures the Italians rank second in percentage of these crimes, being very slightly exceeded by the Greeks....Of blackmail and extortion the Italians also have the highest percentage...the Italians have the highest percentage of homicide. Rape, likewise, forms a higher percentage of the crimes of Italians than of those of any other nationality in the statistics of the New York City's magistrates' Courts, the New York Court of General Sessions, and the penal institutions of Massachusetts. In the County and Supreme Court records of New York State the Italian percentage of rape is second in rank, being very slightly exceeded by the German, while in the Chicago figures, the Greeks report a high percentage. Of all aggregate offenses against public policy, the Italian percentage exceeds all others in two sets of data--those from the New York Court of General Sessions and the County and Supreme Courts of New York State. Of violations of city ordinances shown in the records of the City Magistrates' Courts of Greater New York, the Italian percentage is the greatest, while the same offenses shown in the records of arrests by the Chicago police, the Italian percentage ranks third." (38)

The Immigration Commission also pointed out that the Italians ranked first in percentage of crimes of personal violence in New York City while in Chicago they ranked third behind the Lithuanians and Slavonians. The Commission however, pointed out that the Italians were not among the leaders in percentage of crimes committed against chastity.

(39)   Also among the findings of the Immigration Commission, of the major offenses committed during 1904, the Italians committed the lowest percentage according to race and nationality in burglary, larceny and forgery (40), and were next to the lowest in drunkenness and were the lowest in the offense of vagrancy. (41)

The U.S. Industrial Commission in their reports in 1901 came up with some interesting findings regarding Italian crime.   They found in their hearings that the Italians did not do so poorly in the crime statistics compared with other immigrant groups.   The following is a chart comparing immigrant groups with their rate of commitment to the prisons 1896-1897.

England	0.60 per thousand	
Ireland	2.61 per thousand	
Scotland	0.82 per thousand	
Germany	0.13 per thousand	
Sweden & Norway	0.12 per thousand	
ITALY	0.12 per thousand	
Russia	0.08 per thousand	
Austria	0.04 per thousand	(42)

One of the witnesses to appear before the U.S. Industrial Commission declared that "...the Italians are an orderly and lawfearing class, the cases of the too free use of the knife being too rare exceptions to prove the contrary.   Although their standard of life upon arriving in this country is relatively low, it rises rapidly.   Italian labor is certainly welcome to do the rough work on railroads, sewers, etc., which American laborers are unwilling to undertake." (43)   Another witness pointed out that Italians are rarely found in almshouses. (44)

Eric Sartorio pointed out that Italian women were seldom found in police courts.   Only 8 were deported for "immoral conduct" in 1914 (out of 65,247 Italian women arriving in America).   Among the various groups in New York City, the Italians have one of the smallest percentages of tramps, beggars, and "bums."   Jacob Riis estimated that only 2% of New York City's street beggars were Italian, and Mr. Forbes, president of the Society for the Prevention of Mendicancy in New York, reported that he had never seen or heard of an Italian tramp. (45)   Beck reported that in a study by the Vice Commission in Wisconsin, the Italian women ranked very low in percentage engaged in prostitution.   "...the girls of Italian families are most carefully guarded, and very few become unchaste."   Both parents, especially the father, are deeply concerned with a daughter's morality. "This desire is so strong in the father that he considers himself and family so severely disgraced by any act of immorality on the part of his daughter, that he prefers death to her disgrace." (46)

Grose, in his study of the Italian Americans, made some interesting observations. "Concerning the charge that the Italian is a degenerate, lazy and a pauper, half a criminal, a menace to our civilization, it is shown that in New York the Italians number about 450,000 and the Irish over 300,000. In males, the Italians outnumber the Irish two to one. Consider these facts: In 1904 one thousand five hundred and sixty-four Irish, and only sixteen Italians, were admitted to the almshouse on Blackwell's Island." (47) Grose also showed that in the area of begging, between July 1, 1904 and September 30, 1905, the Medicancy Police in New York City arrested 519 Irish and only 92 Italians. "As to insanity, the figures tell their own story: In the charitable institutions of the country, there were of the insane: Irish 5,943; Germans 4,408; English 1,822; Scandanavians, 1,985; and Italians 718." (48) Grose concluded that Italian crime is grossly exaggerated. (49) "What, then, is the conclusion of our study? On the whole, decidedly favorable to the Italian, while recognizing the vicious and undesirable element that forms a comparatively small part of the whole. The Italian in general is approachable, receptive to American ideas, not criminal by nature more than other races, not difficult to adapt himself to new environment, and eager to learn and learn. He furnishes excellent raw materials for American citizenship, if he does not come too rapidly to be Americanized." (50)

G. LaPiana, in a study of the Italians in Milwaukee, completed in 1915, showed that the extent of Italian crime was vastly overrated. In the period 1910 through 1913, the Italians made up 1.67% of the arrests in that city and many of these arrests were for violating minor ordinances of which they were ignorant and not due to disregard of the laws. LaPiana also found that the Italians ranked low (0.59%) in the area of assault with intent to do bodily harm; burglary (0.64%); contributing to the delinquency of a child (2.22%); disorderly conduct (1.19%); indecent exposure (1.55%); larceny (1.07%); vagrancy (1.09%); willful destruction of property (1.53%); inmates or keeping disorderly houses (0.85%); and drunk and disorderly (0.027%). On the poor side of the ledger, LaPiana found the Italian population made up 48.50% of the arrests for carrying concealed weapons; 27.95% of the arrests for murder; 11.33% of the arrests for those threatening to kill, and 6.89% for those violating city ordinances. (51)

One should bear in mind that at the time these statistics were taken the Italians made up 1.26% of the population of Milwaukee and though they made up 1.67% of the arrests this is not enough case for the exaggerated accusation of high amounts of Italian crime. LaPiana also found in his research that though the Italians made up 1.67% of those arrested they made up 8.68% of those who were discharged after arrest. (52) This is an indication that a great deal of the arrests were probably due to the assumption on the part of many law enforcement officials that the Italian committed the crime. Here again, we see that the extent of Italian crime is overrated and the Italian has a stigma to bear that is grossly unfair.

Over the years the Italian has been accused of being among the most notorious criminals of the various immigrant groups. While the evidence points to the fact that he is not the lowest among the various groups in the committing of crime, he is not the highest. However, he suffers from a bad press and the sensational gangland killings that have occasionally occurred seems to make it extremely difficult for him to overcome the accusations of criminality. These accusations of criminality against the Italian-American have certainly had a harmful effect on the economic opportunities of the Italian-American.

Most of these assumptions need more research but there are indications that the Italian percentage of crime has come down since the first few decades of the twentieth century as the Italian-American has progressed up the economic, political and social ladder in the United States.

Source Notes

(1) Arthur M. Schlesinger, The Rise of the City, 1878-1898 (Chicago: Quadrangle Books, 1971), p. 111. This book was first published in 1933.

(2) Luciano J. Iorizzo and Salvatore Mondello, The Italian-Americans (New York: Twayne Publishers, Inc., 1971), p. 36.

(3) Antonio Mangano, Sons of Italy: A Social and Religious Study of Italians in America (New York: Missionary Education Movement of the United States and Canada, 1917), p. 109.

(4) Philip M. Rose, The Italians in America, with an introduction by Charles Hatch Sears (New York: Charles H. Doran Co., 1922), p. 78.

(5) "Our Future Citizens," New York Times, March 5, 1822, p. 6.

(6) "Our Brigands," New York Times, January 1, 1884, p. 4.

(7) Enrico Sartorio, Social and Religious Life of Italians in America (Boston: The Christopher Publishing House, 1918), pp. 24-25.

(8) Ibid., pp. 30-31.

(9) Leonard Covello, The Social Background of the Italo-American School Child (New York University: Unpublished Doctoral Dissertation, 1944), p. 276.

(10) Ibid., p. 263.

(11) Nathan Glazer and Daniel Patrick Moynihan, Beyond the Melting Pot (Cambridge, Mass.: M.I.T. Press, 1963), p. 195.

(12) Robert Foerster, The Italian Emigration of Our Times (Cambridge: Harvard University Press, 1919), pp. 404-405.

(13) Ibid., pp. 405-406.

(14) "Mafia's Code in New York," New York Times, May 16, 1893, p. 9.

(15) Iorizzo and Mondello, op. cit., pp. 160-164.

(16) Napoleone Calajanni, "Homicide and the Italians," Forum (March, 1901), 62-68.

(17) Arthur Woods, "The Problem of the Black Hand," McClure's Magazine 33 (May, 1909), 40.

(18) Alberto Periconi, "The Italians in the United States," Forum XLV (January, 1911), 19.

(19) Humbert S. Nelli, "Ethnic Group Assimilation: The Italian Experience," Cities in American History, ed. Kenneth T. Jackson and Stanley K. Schultz (New York: Alfred A. Knopf, 1972), pp. 206-208.

(20) William E. Leuehtenburg, The Perils of Prosperity, 1914-32 (Chicago & London: The University of Chicago Press, 1958), p. 216.

(21) New York Times, September 4, 1931, p. 6.

(22) New York Times, September 11, 1931, p. 1.

(23) New York Times, February 16, 1929, p. 1.

(24) Andrew Rolle, The Immigrant Upraised (Norman: The University of Oklahoma Press, 1968), p. 106.

(25) Iorizzo and Mondello, op. cit., p. 6.

(26) Ibid., p. 7.

(27) Humbert S. Nelli, The Italians in Chicago, 1880-1930 (New York: Oxford University Press, 1970), p. 211.

(28) Ibid., p. 212.

(29) Ibid., pp. 218-219.

(30) Ibid., pp. 221-222.

(31) Daniel Bell, The End of Ideology, 2nd. ed. (New York: Collier Books, Inc., 1962), pp. 141-148. See also Daniel Bell, "Crime as an American Way of Life," Antioch Review XIII, No. 2 (Summer, 1953), 131-154.

(32) New York Times, May 13, 1970, p. 45.

(33) New York Times, July 23, 1970, p. 1.

(34) For an excellent study of anti-immigrant attitudes on the part of Americans see John Higham, Strangers in the Land: Patterns of American Nativism, 1860-1925 (New Brunswick: Rutgers University Press, 1955).

(35) Oscar Handlin, Race and Nationality in American Life (Garden City: Doubleday & Company, Inc., 1957), pp. 81-82.

(36) Reports of the Immigration Commission, 1907-1910. 41 vols. Volume II (Washington, D.C.: Government Printing Office, 1911), p. 27.

(37) Reports of the Immigration Commission, 1907-1910. 41 vols. Volume XXXVI (Washington, D.C.: Government Printing Office, 1911), pp. 17-18.

(38) Ibid., pp. 19-20.

(39) Ibid., p. 20.

(40) Ibid., p. 231.

(41) Ibid., p. 232.

(42) U.S. Industrial Commission, Reports of the Industrial Commission on Immigration, Vol. XV (Washington: Government Printing Office, 1901), p. LXX.

(43) Ibid., p. LXIX.

(44) Ibid., p. LXXII.

(45) Sartorio, op. cit., p. 27.

(46) Frank Orman Beck, The Italian in Chicago (Chicago: Chicago Department of Public Welfare Bulletin, February, 1919), p. 27.

(47) Howard Grose, Aliens or Americans? With introduction by Josiah Strong. (New York & Toronto: Young People's Missionary Movement, 1906), p. 139.

(48) Ibid., p. 140.

(49) Ibid., p. 141.

(50) Ibid., p. 150.

(51) G. LaPiana, The Italians in Milwaukee (Milwaukee: The Associated Charities, 1915), pp. 44-57.

(52) Ibid.

Chapter IV

THE ECONOMICS OF THE ITALIAN IMMIGRANT

After 1880, till the United States of America put restrictions on immigration, millions of Italians migrated to America. The great majority of them were from Southern Italy and estimates conclude that more than 80% of them were illiterate. Before going into the reasons for the Italian immigration to this country one must first understand the basic social structure of Southern Italy.

There were two main bases of unity for the Italian in Southern Italy: the extended family and his village. To most southern Italians, people outside their families were considered to be enemies. One could not rely on those outside of the family for assistance. A person's responsibility was limited to the members of the extended family. In a different way, members of a different family living in the same village were to be tolerated. Most Italian families in the villages of Southern Italy felt that they had a bond with each other against their common enemies: the lords, the government and the Catholic Church, all of which they felt exploited them.

During the period from 1870, when Italy became a nation, Italy continued to be an agricultural country, particularly in the south. The conditions of the peasant population in Italy was its greatest source of problems. Agriculture was a lucrative business in the north and the peasants had not been subjected to the unfavorable climate of the south. Land projects, such as irrigation and rural cooperation, contributed to the economic success of Northern Italy. Adverse conditions that led to emigration from Northern Italy were extreme cold at the foothills of the Alps prolonging the non-growing season, unproductive nature of mountain land, inheritances leading to plots too small to cultivate as a result of subdivision, absentee landlordism and heavy taxation. (1)

To look at the reasons for the migration of the Italian from Southern Italy will take longer.

In Southern Italy the primary requirement for success-ful agriculture was lacking. "The rainfall is so slight and virtually absent for such long intervals of time that the richest soils would produce scantily. The situation is worst in Sicily, but serious enough also on the continent. In some years, the summer is almost devoid of rainfall, and the drought may endure for seven months. Though the temperature is seldom higher than during the hot days of a Massachusetts summer, the heat is recurringly great day after day. Whatever rain falls, therefore, quickly evaporates. Within sight of the blue sea the grass of Sicily is a lifeless brown and the road a powder of white.

The plight of agriculture in Italy during the last thirty years of the nineteenth century was a major cause of emigration, especially from the south. After 1871, the pro-duction of olive oil remained the same, while the population of Italy increased by 25%; the production of wine remained sta-tionary after 1885. After 1884, the production of wheat, which occupies the greatest acreage in Italian agriculture, rose about 20 percent, partly under the stimulus since 1888 of a high protective tariff....After 1870, a large increase took place in the production of oranges and lemons, but the prices declined by 65-70 percent. Similar great declines have ruled, since before 1880, in the prices of many other important agricultural products, while the production has in general either remained stationary or declined, and the imports have risen." (3)

Other problems which the Southern Italians suffered from was torrential rains, devasting fever and tremendous earthquakes. In addition, Italy suffered from more malaria than any other European country. The southern provinces of Bascilicata and Calabria had enormous suffering due to malaria. The Southern peasants (contadini) were also oppressed by the large landlords. With the creation of the new national govern-ment in 1870, the Catholic Church lost most of its lands but these lands eventually became part of the landholdings of the wealthy. The absentee landlord and the Sicilian leaseholder ('gabeletto') helped to force poverty and inefficient agriculture upon the Southern peasant. Peasants were working with the same implements that their ancestors used over two thousand years before. More than anything else, the problem of over-population was particularly devastating to the peasant. The landlords and the Italian government felt that they did not have to do anything to improve the conditions of the peasants because there was always an abundant supply of agricultural workers.

For Italy's peasants, the nation's unification in 1870 was a "rivoluzione mancata" or "lost revolution." Instead of helping Italy's poor, the revolution merely passed "the reigns of power to the Italian middle-class which appeared unwilling to assist the poor. The peasants of the 'Mizzagoria' (the South) were determined not to stand by idly while the fruits of victory went mainly to the northerners." Garibaldi's promise to the peasants of land distribution never came about after independence was achieved. "...the 'Risorgimento' was an agrarian-populist revolution which was subverted by Cavour and the liberals." The civil disabilities and poverty endured by the peasants for centuries were thought by many of them as coming to an end; "but by the 1860s their equality before the law, their active participation in the struggle for liberty, and their defense of the new nation through universal conscription had aroused in the peasants new aspirations." They came to America to seek the goals of the 'Risorgimento' which was never achieved in Italy. (4)

Throughout the 19th century, Italian immigration to South America exceeded that into North America. Between 1820 and 1850 less than 4,500 Italians came to the United States. Before 1860 immigration from Italy appears to have been those who desired permanent settlement and came from North Italy. Between 1850 and 1860, 8,940 Italians came to the United States; between 1861 and 1870, 12,206 Italians came; and between 1871 and 1880, 55,759 Italians came to the United States. "Between 1860 and 1880, as the fresh arrivals increased, the immigration assumed a much more definite character. Where before there had been individuals, there were now types and classes. From small beginnings the contingent from South Italy had swelled to substantial proportions. After 1870, for the first time, it became evident that, following a somewhat indeterminate stay, many repacked their chattels and went home again. No previous immigrants into this land of promise had done that!" (5) The small proportion of northern Italians emigrating to the United States, when compared with those emigrating from South Italy (in 1910 about 1 in 6 were from North Italy), in general the unskilled character of the immigration, is not only because of conditions in the old country, "but to the unequal opportunity which America offers to the different classes of Italian society. America has not wanted, save in exceptional trades and professions, the skilled worker or professional man." (6)

During the years of great amounts of emigration to the United States, the proportion of laborers and servants went over sixty percent. During a period of low emigration, like the late 1890s, the amount fell to below forty percent. This shows that rapid economic growth in America did not only bring in more immigrants, but it made available exceptionally large numbers of opportunities for the unskilled worker. (7)

One of the most recent studies of Italian population "...claims that early in the nineteenth century natural increase per annum was of the order of 3/1,000. In the early 1870s, when epidemics and famines had become less destructive, the rate was a little over 6/1,000. A decade later it was 11/1,000, for the death-rate fell from 30/1,000 to under 20/1,000 in the forty years before the Great War, while the birth-rate began to fall significantly only halfway through that period. Even with massive emigration, Italy's population rose by more than six million between 1880 and 1910; for an excess of births of some 200,000 in the late 1870s turned into one of 350,000 a quarter of a century later." (8)

To the poor peasant from Southern Italy, America was a land of hope. In the last decade of the nineteenth century, an American consul, inquiring about the causes of emigration from Naples, said that he was always told, "My friend in America is doing well and he has sent for me." (9) Not only did American laborers earn more than their Italian counter-parts, but their wages had more purchasing power. "Meat, which was virtually essential to the American workingman, was beyond the means of his equal in Italy." Natural disasters such as earthquakes, volcanoes and floods, and diseases such as malaria, phylloxera and pellagra "deepened the despair of South Italians." Many Italians felt that natural disaster and disease was a message from God to leave their homeland. Some merely wanted to leave to escape parental authority or com-pulsory military service. Upon arriving in the United States, the great majority of Italians settled mainly in cities because of the economic opportunities which they provided, as well as the excitements of urban life and the many conveniences it pro-vided (running water, indoor toilets, etc.). (10) It was very easy for the padrone (labor boss) and agents of steamship companies to wander up and down the Italian countryside looking for human labor to bring to the United States. "Serv-ing industry, but motivated by the desire for an individual profit, was the padrone. Such a man established a network of personal contacts in his own country, recruited workers who bound themselves to him for a year, advanced their passage money for America, and secured it by having their fathers or other relatives give him a mortgage on their property, for a much larger sum. The system was to be found late in the nineteenth century, in Italy and Greece." (11)

Though one can conclude that the main cause of Italian migration was economic, it was not the only cause. The noted historian, Frederick Jackson Turner, said:

He who believes that even the hordes of recent immigrants from Southern Italy are drawn to these shores by nothing more than a dull and blind materialism has not penetrated into the heart of the problem. The idealism and expectation of these children of the Old World, the hopes which they have found for a newer and freer life across the seas, are almost pathetic when one considers how far they are from the possibility of fruition. He who would take stock of American democracy must not forget the accumulation of human purposes and ideals which immigration has added to the American populace. (12)

However, as stated before, economics was the chief cause of Italian migration to the United States. The appetite of Italians for America was wetted by stories of Italians who had traveled to America and returned home. (13) In 1880, only 28 pounds of meat was consumed by the average Italian each year, while the average American led the world with a consumption of 120 pounds per individual. (14)

In 1874, $260 million in taxes were collected in Italy, while expenditures amounted to $279 million, leaving a deficit of $19 million. The public debt at the end of 1874 was almost $2 billion, "and the total charges on the account of the public debt, in the expenditure of the year," totalled over $146 million. Italy's crippling taxation could not meet her lavish expenditures. (15) In an article published later in the same year the New York Times pointed out that nineteen and one-half percent of the Italian government's income "was derived from taxing the most common necessities of living, such as breadstuffs, meats, and salt." A typical farm of Italian laborers paid 80 lire annually in taxes, while the same family in France pays only 11.50f." In France, the average yearly wage for laborers was 1200f., while in Italy it was 669f. "...there is a tax on landed property which amounts to 126,000,000 lire, and this is in itself felt as a heavy burden on agriculture, in which, of course, the laborer shares. Again the lottery from which 70,000,000 lire is derived, is practically almost as direct a tax on the poor as that of breadstuffs...." (16)

Italy's desire to become a first-rate power after she became unified in 1870 had its effect on the peasantry of Italy. "The poor everywhere are all crushed by heavy taxes for maintenance of the large army and navy which made Italy a first-class European power. More serious than the exaction of the tax-gatherer is the long-continued agricultural depression that has reduced a large part of the South to poverty." (17)

Another important reason why the Italians were able to migrate to the United States was because of the improvements in transportation. With the development of the steamship, the immigrant was able to come to the United States in a little more than a week by 1900. The new era of international relations ushered in after 1870 emphasized the importance of great navies and great merchant fleets seemed to be necessary complements. "England, France, Germany, and Italy hurried to build up their tonnage. Toward that end they were willing to grant heavy subsidies to the operators of the lines bearing their flags. Under those circumstances the price of steerage passage on a steamship fell to as little as twelve dollars, and included food...steam had displaced sail in the emigrant-carrying business....Comfort and safety increased also." (18)

Steamship lines hired subagents "throughout Europe who made a living on the commissions from the sale of steam-ship tickets, and thus found it to their own interest to spread the tidings of America....[They] stood at Italian church doors distributing cards with hymns and verses praising the United States." (19)

Though the Italian peasants took up the call to go to America, they emigrated with the intent of eventually return-ing to their homeland with enough money to live comfortably. Because of this the first Italian immigrants to come to the United States after 1870 were mainly men, who desired to return to their native village in Italy after working in the United States for a few years and making their fortune. However, since most of the men were unskilled laborers, they found that they had to work for minimal wages. Therefore, most of them were not able to save enough to return to Italy and live comfortably. They found that only with a great effort could they make enough to send enough money back to Italy to bring the rest of their family.

The Italian immigrant not only had a strong desire to return home but he had the desire to help those at home. In 1907, the Immigrant Commission estimated that "...$18,500,000 in remittances found its way across the Atlantic to Italy." This helped in creating "a favorable, if not roseate, picture of America." (20) The high rate of returns among the Italians led to much anti-Italian feeling in the United States. In order to fully understand the rate of return to Italy one must take a look at the statistics of the period.

In the decade of 1891-1900 over 655,000 Italian immigrants came to the United States. In the same decade approximately 220,000 Italians emigrated from the United States. In the decade of 1901-1910 over 2,045,000 Italian immigrants came to the United States while over 1,154,000 Italians returned to Italy. In the decade of 1911-1920 over 1,109,000 Italian immigrants came to the United States while over 911,000 Italians emigrated from the United States. (21) The Italians had a high rate of return because "...groups with a high proportion of men were especially prone to a high rate of return, whether because of easy response to fluctuations in employment or because of intentionally seasonal migration." (22) A contemporary observer stated that "...the very poverty and lack of capital among the peasantry, coupled with the intensive love of country which nearly every Italian feels for his native land, explains why so many Italians return to Italy after having sojourned for awhile in a foreign land. The savings of his exile enable him to establish himself in comfort among his more genial native surroundings, as a small capitalist and landowner, and his example, in turn, sends his friends abroad to seek their fortune too." (23) However, we know that the latter observer was stating more of the hopes than the actualities that occurred.

Mass migration from Italy did not start until after 1870. From that time onward, the Italian migration became modern history's greatest and most continuous movement of population from a single country. The Immigration Committee found that:

> More than half a million Italians have emigrated in certain years since 1900 to different parts of the world. About one-half of this emigration is to other European countries and is temporary in character, being composed mostly of men. From 1889 to 1910 inclusive, 2,284,601 Italian immigrants were admitted to the United States and a large number also emigrated from Italy to South American countries. A large part of those who come to the United States return to their former homes. The net gain, however, especially in New York and other States of the East, is large. The South Italian immigrants numbered more than 240,000 in 1907--that is, more than half as many again as the next highest immigrant race. The North Italians send only about one-fifth as many. (24)

The Immigration Commission further reported that by 1910 over 1,000,000 Italians migrated to Brazil; over 620,000 migrated to Argentina, over 140,000 migrated to other parts of South America; and over 60,000 migrated to Africa from the Italian Peninsula. (25)

The Immigration Commission also found that the heaviest amount of Italian immigrants came from the southern provinces of Sicily and Calabria "the least productive and most poorly developed portions of the country. Very few emigrate from Sardinia. The compartimento of Liguria, the home of the Genoese, also South Italians in race, contributed more emigrants than any other province in northern Italy." (26)

During the first two decades of the twentieth century immigration to the United States was very high in general, and in the period from 1905 to 1915 nearly 12,000,000 immigrants came to the United States. (27) During the period from 1901 to 1920 over 3,150,000 Italian immigrants came to the United States. (28) Between the years of 1906 and 1915 the emigration from southern Italy was so great that the net loss in population of Calabria was 40%, in Basilicata it was 38.5% and in the combined regions of Abruzzo-Molise the loss reached 43%. (29) Between 1871 and 1921 almost 4,300,000 Italians entered the United States. (30)

In the beginning of the mass migration from Italy, the Italian government did not view with favor the permanent migration of its people and tried various means to discourage the emigration from Italy. In March of 1880 the New York Times reported a dispatch from the London Telegraph.

According to a statement just published, the Italian Government, alarmed at the increase in the emigration from the Peninsula to an average of fully 130,000 persons annually, has issued a special circular to the Prefects, recommending 'stronger measures' to stop the stream than they have hitherto adopted. Of what nature are these measures we have not yet been informed, but it may safely be predicted that nothing short of force will avail to keep the would-be emigrants at home....There are facilities for the spread of information now which did not exist a few years ago, and it is impossible to keep the Italians quite in the dark as to keep them contented with their life of privation at home. To dissuade them from going by the help of obstacles interposed by the Prefects will only irritate and must fail. The remedy must go

deeper. If Italian statesmen would cut down their
military and naval establishments, and lighten the load
of taxation, they would do something to tempt the
people to remain at home. (31)

However, once the Italian government saw that they
could not do anything to stop the vast hordes of Italians from
emigrating from their homeland, they accepted it and tried to
help the immigrants.

Before the turn of the twentieth century, the Italian
central government concentrated its public works projects and
educational aid in the more prosperous North, rather than the
South where such things were really needed. Though the
first years of the twentieth century brought much needed
reform in agriculture, education, labor relations, as well as
the passage of social legislation, "it should be noted that this
period corresponded with the crest of the outward wave of
emigrants who, mindful of the past, despaired of the government's ability to create an acceptable economic milieu and
sojourned abroad in quest of economic betterment." This
massive migration worked to Italy's advantage however, as
"remittances from foreign lands helped shore the sagging
finances of government, corporations, and individuals." The
emigration acted as a safety valve. "relieving the nation's
unemployment problem and helping to raise wages for those
who remained behind. (32)

So often the journey to leave their village and come to
a new land is overlooked. Taylor gives a look at a Sicilian
emigrants' journey to Naples and shows it as an illustration of
the universal conflict between enlightened law and human
incompetence or greed.

Emigrants began by obtaining birth-certificates, which
were sent by the village shoemaker, the local ticket
agent, to Messina, where police checked for liability to
military service, and then issued a passport. Only
then could a ticket be sold. Departure was long
prepared. Baggage was packed. Prayers for a safe
journey were offered at a special service. Farewell
calls were paid and family graves visited. A dance
and an evening serenade were part of the ritual. At
last, baggage was sent in carts to the nearest railway
station, then the emigrants themselves, walking or
riding donkeys, set off. The train carried them to
Messina, where a Customs inspection took place, and
where everyone passed through an agent's office to

answer questions for a declaration form, corresponding to the questions American officials would ask. Already, however, spurious medical certificates could be seen on sale. Rowing boats, whose crews insisted on tips, took them out to a small and dirty steamer. After many hours without food, they reached Naples, where they were left for a long time in the blazing sun. The shipping line then issued ration-tickets, and, after another Customs inspection, all were sent to a licensed hotel, then to a restaurant for a meal of soup, stew, melon and wine, accosted as they walked by hawkers. Embarkation day saw bustle and confusion. After examination by an American consular official, the heavy baggage was carefully recorded and placed in the ship's hold. Men were selling grass ropes, to tie up bags which were already falling apart. Hand luggage was supposed to be taken in a small steamboat across the harbor for fumigation, but men were at hand to sell spurious labels and seals. Vaccination was then called for, but, again, certificates could be bought. Medical inspection by a port doctor, the ship's surgeon, and an American doctor from the Marine Hospital Corps was the last formal event, though sometimes a further check was made on board to ensure that documents procured by a fit man had not been transferred at the last minute to someone who was diseased. Emigrants then went on board, carrying baggage and rush-bottomed chairs bought at twenty cents for use on deck. Bumboats were thick along the ship's side, selling fruit, pipes, hats, medicines and lucky charms. (33)

By the beginning of the twentieth century the transportation became easier and better as the ships improved. An example of an Italian ship that brought immigrants to the United States was the vessel 'Tomaso di Savoia,' which was built by Barclay Curle.

Only 450 feet long, she measured 7,914 gross tons. Her rather more than one hundred First-class passengers had a dining-saloon, smoking-room, music-room, 'winter garden,' and nursery. The hundred Second-class had dining-saloon only. Her 1,200 steerage had only two tiny dining-saloons, the larger measuring no more than twenty-eight feet by twenty-four feet. Galley and bakery, however, were more ample than in some other ships studied, and 'sale shop' and 'bread shop' are marked on the plan. The seven steerage compartments were on two decks; and stairways led to two blocks containing together eight showers, twenty wash-basins, eighteen W.C.s, and urinals. Eight wash-tubs were provided, and a laundry was situated in the forward deck-house. All in all, one is surprised at how much could be provided in so small a ship, and how completely the 1901 statute was being observed. Apart from laundry, the plan shows hospital accommodation, with separate space for infectious diseases. Among the First-class luxury suites is one for the 'commissario regio,' one room fitted with brass bedstead. Next to the radio cabin is a chaplain's room, representing a quick response to a papal decision of 1906, to provide for emigrants' spiritual needs. (34)

Though the movement of the Italians to the United States was not easy, in the long view the Italian who came looking for economic opportunities, as did most other immigrants of the same period, did also serve to benefit the economy and the urbanization of the United States. Between 1870 and 1920, the United States made tremendous strides, both industrially and financially. This was especially the case in the urban areas of the northeast. The Italian immigrant chose in great part to settle in these urban areas and leave his agricultural heritage to the past.

Before the period of the great Italian migration to the United States, the pattern of their settlement in cities east of the Mississippi River and north of the Ohio River was started by northern Italians who founded an immigrant community. The north Italians tended to predominate until the 1880s. "The original enclave started in or near the center city--that is, the business area--and was characterized by the movement of economically successful newcomers out of the ethnic district and into the wider American community. New arrivals from overseas swarmed into the colony, filling vacancies and creating or contributing to overcrowded, rapidly deteriorating neighborhoods." (35) Of the Italian immigrants who became permanent residents of the United States, less than 10% entered agricultural occupations even though more than 75% of them had been formerly peasant farmers. (36)

The Italians located themselves in metropolitan areas because of the job opportunities available there; the skill or training which the immigrant brought with him was useful there; and because of the location of family or friends. Italians settled in manufacturing or mining centers located in the New England area through the middle Atlantic States and in the East North Central region (Ohio, Michigan, Illinois). Outside of these areas, San Francisco and New Orleans were the only prominent areas of settlement by Italian immigrants. (37) The United States Industrial Committee, in a study, found that in 1890, 59% of all Italian immigrants settled in the cities. "In other words, the more illiterate races tend to the cities in a greater degree than the others. This fact is attributed by the witness to the lack of enterprise and energy on the part of these races. There are plenty of unsettled regions in the country to which Italians could go if they would, but they have not the disposition. They do not even go south where they might seem to be invited by the climate." (38)

Evidence of the urbanization of the Italian immigrant can be found in the following information shown by Professor Charles Coulter in 1919. Three-sevenths of the Italian population in Maryland was found in Baltimore; 5/6 of the Italian population in Delaware was found in Wilmington; 3/8 of the Italian population in Illinois was found in Chicago; 2/3 of the Italian population in Nebraska was found in Omaha; 3/5 of the Italian population in Missouri was found in St. Louis; 1/2 of the Italian population in Oregon was found in Portland; 2/5 of the Italian population in Louisiana was found in New Orleans; 1/3 of the Italian population in Michigan was found in Detroit; and 1/2 of the Italian population in Ohio was found in Cleveland. New York City was next to Naples, the largest Italian city in the world. According to Coulter, 78.1% of the Italians in the United States lived in urban centers while only 21.9% lived in rural communities, "a fact which may indicate the unwillingness of these immigrants from rural Italy, accustomed by tradition and training to agriculture, to pursue their agricultural occupation here. America seems to mean for them the deliverance from everything connected with the tilling of the soil." (39)

Cleveland was the center of Italian life in Ohio. The Italian immigrants had their first residences in that city and later branched out into the neighboring towns. "Owing to the convergence of this population into restricted areas from which other nationalities are substantially excluded, the second generation, native born of foreign parents, are reared in what is practically an Italian colony, where the mother tongue is spoken. Italian traditions, ideals, and customs are perpetuated and a national solidarity is maintained. In these Italian blocks the children are bilingual, the parochial and even the public schools are almost exclusively of Italian composition." (40)

The Italian pattern of settlement in the city of Chicago was generally typical of the experience of Italian settlement in American cities. The first Italian settlers in Chicago came from Northern Italy, from Tuscany and Genoa, in the years following 1850. The newcomers, regardless from what part of Italy they came, first settled on the same streets and in the same tenement houses that others from the same province had settled earlier. They then looked for employment in the same places where others from their province worked. "This early concentration broke down as the immigrants met and mingled with newcomers from other towns and provinces and with non-Italians who lived and worked in close proximity." While this was happening, the Italian immigrants, for the first time started to think of themselves as Italians, instead of belonging to a particular family. "Whereas in Sicily and southern Italy, life centered around family needs and goals; in the United States the family was neither large enough nor sufficiently powerful to ensure aid in all emergencies. Hence in this new world a community identity and an ethnic consciousness evolved, one that bore little resemblance to the family-dominated society of the Italian South. Rather than being an importation, this community feeling and awareness of being Italian developed in the United States as a response to changed surroundings." (41)

An observer, writing in 1881, described, in not very complimentary terms, the Italians in New York City. "The more recently arrived herd together in colonies, such as those in Baxter and Mott Streets, in Eleventh Street, in Yorkville, and in Hoboken. Many of the most important industries of the city are in the hands of Italians as employers and employed, such as the manufacture of macaroni, of objects of art, confectionery, artificial flowers; and Italian workmen may be found everywhere mingled with those of other nationalities. It is no uncommon thing to see at noon some swarthy Italian, engaged on a building in process or erection, resting and dining from his tin kettle, while his brown-skinned wife sits by his side, brave in her gold earrings and beads, with a red flower in her hair, all of which at home were kept for feast days." (42)

Another observer, writing in 1894, stated that Italians go to Italian quarters as soon as they reach America.

As soon as an Italian lands in America he hastens to the Italian quarter and there he is likely to stay. He finds men and women who speak his own language. He lodges with an Italian, eats at an Italian restaurant;

stores kept by his countrymen supply all his wants.
Bankers, employment agents, lawyers, interpreters,
physicians, musicians, artisans, laborers, grocers,
bakers, butchers, barbers, merchants, are all there, a
town within a town. Hence the "Italian quarter" has
great cohesive force. Now it seems plain that even if
we cannot dissolve the nucleus that is already formed
we should keep it from growing larger....There is but
one way in which this can be done, and that is by
colonization. The remedy for centralization is decen-
tralization. (43)

Another observer, writing in the early part of the
twentieth century, noted that four-fifths of the Italians in New
York City come from areas of less than 10,000 population. He
called the Italian settlements "as cities within a city." The
Italians in New York City, according to this observer, were a
collection of small villages and they kept all the characteristics
of village life.

In one street will be found peasants from one Italian
village; in the next street the place of origin is different and distinct, and different and distinct are manners, customs and sympathies. Entire villages have
been transplanted from Italy to one New York street,
and with the others have come the doctor, the grocer,
the priest, and the annual celebration of the local
patron saint. The acute rivalry between village
people, who have not developed and can scarcely be
expected to develop in a short period what may be
called "city consciousness," is perhaps the most important cause of the lack of coherence in the Italian mass,
which makes impossible united and persistent effort on
its part in any direction, economic, social or political.
(44)

This observer also pointed out that in the Italian
quarter in New York City the life is centered around the tenement. "The families are usually large, and in most of them
boarders are taken with a view to eking out the payment of
the rent. There are tenements occupied by Italians in New
York in which eight and ten men sleep in one room, with not
more than 1,500 cubic feet of air to breathe, for eight or nine
hours. Very often a whole family occupies a single sleeping
room, children over fourteen years of age sleeping with their
parents or with smaller brothers and sisters. The first conse-
quence of this overcrowding is an astonishing decline in physical strength." (45)

Things were not much better in the city of Milwaukee, in which an observer in 1915 called the housing "...old, dilapidated and insanitary....The stables are numerous, often adjoining the houses, and, especially in summer, breeding swarms of flies and insects. Four times as many people as should be permitted, are often crowded into a given space. Considering this, the fact is clear that the unhygienic condition of the district, populated almost exclusively by the Italians, is brought about not entirely through faults of their own. The streets, being the center of the traffic, are muddy in winter and dusty in summer; here the children play. The air is heavy and unhealthy with vapors from the lake and river, smoke from chimneys and trains, gas from tanks, odors and insects from the stables, and the crowding together of a population of workmen who often have no conveniences for cleanliness." (46) The same observer found that 40% of the Italian families in Milwaukee took in boarders in order to help pay the rent. (47) The observer went on to explain some of the problems that the taking in of boarders presented.

In Sicily it is dangerous and sometimes almost impossible for a stranger to become very intimate in any household, because jealousy and suspicion are so common among the Sicilians. But in American cities, the necessity of life in common, their restricted social pleasures and continual contact, make such intimacy comparatively easy for the boarder. Men accustomed to family life who have no outside diversion, find the temptation difficult to resist, and there is rarely a case of a boarder whose wife is still in Italy and who is living in a house with young women, that has not had serious consequences; families have been ruined and faithful wives in Italy have been abandoned. (48)

Phillip M. Rose observed that "Necessity, ignorance of the danger involved, and the desire to save throw the newly arrived Italian immigrants into the slums or poorest quarters of great cities and into houses which are run down, ill-adapted to tenement uses, and quite generally flimsy in comparison with the substantial structures of their native town." (49) Rose further pointed out the various problems that Italians living in the tenements faced: the occupation of 2-3 rooms by a household 2-3 times the size of an American one; strain and stress laid upon the mother; the confinement of the women due to Italian superstition; lack of proper ventilation and heating; habitual doubling up of families; of the taking in of lodgers; and minimal bathing. (50)

Adolfo Rossi, writing in the last part of the nineteenth century, told of the poor quality of life he found among the South Italians.

Country folk they had been in Italy, but now they inhabited the dirtiest part of New York City, dwelling often more than one family to a room. 'Men, women, dogs, cats, and monkeys eat and sleep together in the same hole without air and without light.' They buy stale beer at two cents a pint from a rascally Italian in a basement, and they break into endless brawls. During the summer they work on the railroads and in the fields; 'in the winter they return to fill the streets of New York, where the boys are bootblacks and the men either are employed at the most repulsive tasks, scorned by workmen of other nationalities--carrying offal to the ships and dumping it in the sea, cleaning the sewers et similia--or they go about with sacks on their shoulders rummaging the garbage cans, gleaning paper, rags, bones, broken glass.' The Five Points are the center of that species of slavery exercised by Italian bosses or padroni. These fellows know English, hire workmen in herds (being paid by the employers), charge them enormous commissions, having already advanced to many their passage money for the journey from Italy, sell them the necessaries at high prices, and deduct heavy commissions from the savings which they transmit to Italy. (51)

John Foster Carr, an observer writing in the first decade of the twentieth century, commented on the great difficulty of the Italians trying to live in the city.

But there are limits to the building of an Italian city on American soil. New York tenement-houses are not adapted to life as it is organized in the hill villages of Italy, and a change has come over every relation of life. The crowded living is strange and depressing; instead of work accompanied by song in orangeries and vineyards, there is silent toil in the canons of a city street;...there is the rough force of the New York policeman to represent authority. There is the diminished importance of the church, and, in spite of their set ways, there is different eating and drinking, sleeping and waking. A different life breeds different habits, and different habits with American surroundings effect a radical change in the man. It is difficult for the American to realize this.

He sees that the signs and posters of the colony are all in Italian; he hears the newsboys cry 'Progresso,' 'Araldo,' 'Bolletino'; he hears peddlers shout out in their various dialects the names of strange-looking vegetables and fish. The whole district seems so Italianized and cut off from the general American life that it might as well be one of the ancient walled towns of the Apennines. He thinks that he is transported to Italy, and moralizes over the 'unchanging colony.' But the greenhorn from Fiumefreddo is in another world. Everything is strange to him; and I have repeatedly heard Italians say that for a long time after landing they could not distinguish between an Italian who had been here four or five years and a native American. (52)

Because of the difficult conditions that the Italian found himself in upon arriving in the United States he was subjected to some allegations that one would hardly call complimentary. Jacob Riis, the noted newspaperman, called the Italian a gambler and an unsanitary person who "whenever the back of the sanitary police is turned, he will make his home in the filthy burrow where he works by day, sleeping and eating his meals under the dump." (53)

The Italian immigrant upon entering the United States had to begin work almost immediately because he usually had little money with him. He, therefore, went to friends and relatives in the "Little Italy" section of the city and stayed with them until he found employment and could shift for himself. "The reason the percentage of Italian farmers remained small was not their resistance to all efforts by others to better their lot; nor, in most cases, was it because they preferred city labor. Mostly it was a matter of practical economics. When the immigrant came over, he usually had only enough money to last him a few days. He needed work which would give him immediate pay, whether or not in other circumstances it would have been his first choice. Only industrial work met this condition." (54)

The Immigration Commission (Dillingham Commission), meeting in the first decade of the twentieth century, concluded that among the new immigration of which the Italians had the greatest number, "...pauperism...is relatively at a minimum, owing to the fact that the present immigration law provides for the admission only of the able-bodied, or dependents whose support by relatives is assured." (55) The Commission also found that "...in seven cities--New York, Philadelphia,

Chicago, Boston, Cleveland, Buffalo, Milwaukee--a very careful study was made of the conditions prevailing in the poorer quarters of the city inhabited by immigrants of various races. As was to be expected, many extremely pitiful cases of poverty and overcrowding were found, at times six or even more people sleeping in one small room, sometimes without light or direct access by window or door to the open air." (56) The Commission also came to the conclusion that "a large proportion of the southern and eastern European immigrants of the past twenty-five years have entered the manufacturing and mining industries of the eastern and middle western States, mostly in the capacity of unskilled laborers." (57)

The Italian immigrant was hampered in improving the various "Little Italies" of New York City and the many small industrial communities near the city into a single cohesive ethnic group because of the great amount of illiteracy found among the Italians. The differences in dialect engendered much mutual suspicion which continued to endure because of the lack of widespread communication. "The Italian Press was hampered not only by the illiteracy of its clientele but also by the existence of a great gap between the ordinary spoken language and the official language of the press." (58)

Glazer and Moynihan point out that the first Italian neighborhoods remained quite stable. In New York City, neighborhoods in East Harlem which sent LaGuardia to Congress in the 1920s and Marcantonio in the 1940s, sent Alfred Santangelo in the late 1950s and early 1960s. (59) Glazer and Moynihan take the position that Italian districts have remained steady, they don't change much in New York City. "Nor are these old Italian neighborhoods only shells of their former selves, inhabited exclusively by the older people. Many of the married sons and daughters have stayed close to their parents. Even the trek to the suburbs, when it does occur among Italians, is very often a trek of families of two generations, rather than simply of the young." (60)

Professor Humbert S. Nelli in his later study of the Italians, with emphasis on the city of Chicago, comes to different conclusions about the movement of Italians than did Glazer and Moynihan.

Continuing the pattern set by their predecessors, southern Italians and Sicilians who obtained the financial means moved away from the colony. Commenting on the later group, a long-time (German-born) resident of the lower north side noted in 1928 that 'the good Italians have moved up north and out west, and it is only the rough class that remains along Division Street.' If migration from the ethnic settlement--a sign of economic mobility and the indication of desires for better housing and living conditions--did not take place in the first generation, it generally did in the second and third. Nevertheless, the continued presence of numbers of Italians in neighborhoods led contemporaries to the erroneous conclusion (not corrected by present-day scholars) that Italians, their children and their grandchildren after them, remained on the same streets and in the same tenements from the time they arrived in the city until they died, and that compact unchanging settlements grouped according to place of immigrant origin. While this description might have fitted the first phase of settlement, now relationships quickly formed both with other Italians and with members of different nationality groups. A major cause of this constant regrouping and expanding of relationships was the fact that the composition of Italian colonies (as well as of other ethnic groups) was in constant flux, with at least half the community residents changing their place of dwelling each year. (61)

Another view which is different from Glazer and Moynihan is that taken by Gilbert Osofsky in his study Harlem: The Making of a Ghetto, in which he points out that between World War I and the Depression, of the Italian population in Harlem, many moved away as the Negroes moved in. (62) However, Herbert Gans, in his study of the Italians in the West End of Boston, comes to conclusions similar to Glazer and Moynihan. (63)

The correct conclusion is probably somewhere in between the two points of view. The Italians move when their economic and educational conditions improve, as other immigrant groups also move. However, it seems from various studies that Italians do not move away from their original neighborhoods as quickly as some other ethnic groups.

Antonio Mangano, writing in the second decade of the twentieth century, made some observations about Italian's settlement. He noted that few Italians were engaged in mining, but those who were tended to live in small communities isolated from any American settlement. In West Virginia, the city of Fairmont was a center of Italian population with 15,000 Italians living there. Most intelligent Italians worked at the glass works and as merchants. The poor Italians worked in the mines. Mangano noticed a low morality among single men and excessive gambling and drinking. Mangano also observed that few Italian men knew English, became citizens or were interested in politics. He also noted that these Italian mine workers were influenced by the Industrial Workers of the World since, among other things, they were victims of the company store which often furnished low quality food. (64)

In most cities the Italian immigrant faced high rents and irregular employment which posed problems for them. They sought the cheapest shelter and tried to save money. Language barriers prevented the Italian from going outside his community and getting jobs outside the factory or work gang. Until he was able to learn the language, the Italian felt that he must accept his lot. Because of these feelings (and grouping together) he was accused of clannishness and of ignorance (because of his lack of facility in English). (65)

Frank Orman Beck did a special study on the Italians in Chicago during the second decade of the twentieth century which sheds light on the Italian pattern of settlement.

According to the public school census of May, 1914 the Italian population of Chicago was 108,160. However, second generation Italians often gave their nationality as "American," and therefore the correct figure would be over 150,000. The Italians were located in 17 separate neighborhoods of varying sizes. Sixty percent resided in four wards--17th, 19th, 22nd and 1st. (66)

The 17th Ward was the purest Italian neighborhood. It was located just west of the Chicago River; Division Street on the north; Ashland Avenue on the west; Kinzie Street on the south. Five different immigrant groups settled there. The first immigrants, the Irish, started arriving in the late 1850s. The Norwegians arrived in the 17th Ward about the time of the Chicago fire (1871). After the Columbian Exposition in 1893 they began migrating to the area of Logan Square and Humboldt District. Italians arriving from north Italy came about 1890. Southern Italians came later (after 1900). In 1899 the Norwegian Lutheran Church became the Italian Catholic Church. Only 24% of the Italians in Chicago were Northern Italians, the remainder were Southern Italians. Ventilation in apartments of the 17th Ward were described as "far from adequate." "Forty-nine percent of all persons in the area were sleeping in rooms with less than the minimum of legal air required." (67)

In a study of 24 dwellings in the 1st Ward, a bathtub was not found in any of them. In the study of 24 dwellings, infant mortality was extremely high. Of the children born into these 24 families, 42% died in infancy. "If it is true that any condition of housing, which in itself tends to impair the physical or moral health of the tenant, is bad housing, then the housing of the four Italian districts should be so designated."

> Here are dark, damp, disease-breeding basements; tenements with poor fire protection and inadequate plumbing; tenements with no provision or poor provision for heating; overcrowding with people sleeping in cubicles and living in rooms with dwarf partitions; life existing day and night without adequate provisions for fresh and pure air.
> And these overcrowded, unsanitary houses are on overcrowded lots, many of which are so far below the level of the street that they become catch basins for all sorts of refuse and are not infrequently covered with water and always they are damp and disease breeding. (68)

Beck also claimed that the diet of the Italian in Chicago was definitely superior to that of his native homeland. "The Italian's diet in Chicago is fitted largely for the lighter kind of manual labor only." They ate little meat, but consumed green vegetables, of which they were quite fond, as a substitute. They did not like potatoes, and used little butter, "and still less milk." Fruits and vegetables were "not infrequently purchased in bad condition." The Italian's food was often poorly cooked. Meat and eggs, being fried in lard, became "indigestible and innutritious....The Russian Jew, on the other hand, by long, slow cooking makes a palatable and nutritious dish of his chuck beef, and even lower cuts of meat." Children were fed a great deal of black coffee and butterless bread, but did not receive enough wholesome, mineral rich food. (69)

Beck gave a favorable report on how the Italians kept their homes. "They endeavor to achieve the imposing. Barring this fact and considering the types of apartments occupied, and with the facilities for housekeeping, Italian housewives compare favorably with other women. In fact, in sections of the city where the Italians live with Polish, Irish and even American neighbors, the Italian apartment is conspicuous for its cleanliness and orderliness. Among even the lowest type of Italian tenants are to be found clean window curtains and in some corner of the room, or some room in the apartment, there are touches of cleanliness, color, or display which reveal the simple effort of the Italian to express his artistic temperament. (70)

The Dillingham Commission concluded that the South Italians are found to have "more than three-fourths of their households, as having spent the entire period of residence since the establishing of the family in the United States, in the neighborhood where they now reside, usually a colony of their race." (71)

The Dillingham Commission, in studying Italian households in the cities of Boston, Buffalo, Chicago, Cleveland, Milwaukee, New York City, and Philadelphia came up with the following information:

Table I*

	Total # of House-holds	Avg. # of Rooms Per Apart-ment	Percent of Households Occupying Apartments of Each Specified Number of Rooms						
			1	2	3	4	5	6	7+
North Italians	77	4.26	1.3	5.2	15.6	45.5	14.3	13.0	5.2
South Italians	1,980	3.28	3.3	23.2	36.9	23.3	7.7	3.7	1.7

* Reports of the Immigration Commission, 1907-1910, 41 vols. (Washington, D.C.: Government Printing Office, 1911) XXVI, p. 31.

Table II*

Average Number of Boarders or Lodgers Per
Household in Same Cities

	Total Number of House- holds-	Number of House- holds Keeping Boarders or Lodgers	Number of Boarders or Lodgers	Avg. Number of Boarders "or Lodgers" Per Household	
				Based on Total # of House- holds	Based on # of House- holds Keep- ing Boarders or Lodgers
North Italians	77	33	89	1.16	2.70
South Italians	1,980	444	1,008	.51	2.27

*   Reports of the Immigration Commission, 1907-1910, 41 vols.
    (Washington, D.C.: Government Printing Office, 1911)
    XXVI, p. 92.

As one can see from the above tables, conditions in
the Italian areas of these seven large cities were very
crowded.

Humbert S. Nelli, in his book, The Italians in
Chicago, 1880-1930, points to studies by the Commissioner of
Labor in 1892-93, and the City Homes Association in 1901, in
which conditions in the district bounded by Halsted,
Newberry, State, Polk and Twelfth Streets, a large Italian

area of population, was studied. "The Commissioner reported serious overcrowding in tenements, high rents for inferior housing, barely adequate sanitary conditions, and extremely poor social relationships. The City Homes Association in 1901 found much tenement-house property to be old and in need of repair, for many residences remained in 'a wretched and dangerous state of dilapidation.' Inhabitants often could not keep such houses clean; consequently, said the report, filth and vermin were to be found everywhere. Crime, squalor, poor hygiene, evil associations, and the collapse of family life resulted from these conditions." (72)

An observer of the Italian scene in the second decade of the twentieth century said:

Now for the first time in his life he comes to live in a big city....Do you expect him to know about hygiene, physical geography, and changes of climate? ...How can he know that there is a difference between canned goods and fresh vegetables? Thus, through ignorance of the new surroundings in which he finds himself, he lives a dog's life and some money is saved. Does he gesticulate, talk loudly, sing in the streets, sit on the sidewalk, to the great amazement and horror of the American-bred in the big city? Think of his village, of his life there, and you will find out why he does it. (73)

Sartorio also observed that among the Italian man's first contacts in this country was the saloon keeper and the ward politician. The saloon keeper taught English to many Italian immigrants. The local politician provided neighborhood gambling houses for the newcomers, and engaged in the "buy-ing" of immigrant votes. Sixty-five percent of the Italian immigrants never voted in Italy, and "the majority of the peasants that come here...do not know the value or clearly understand the use of the vote." (74)

For most of the Italian immigrants the problem of adjusting to the style of life in the United States took place in their own ethnic community. This was not always a big help. Sartorio said: "One of the greatest surprises of my life and one from which I cannot recover, is to hear from time to time, especially from Italian women who have lived in America for years, a statement like this: 'I have been down to America today,' meaning that they have gone a few blocks outside the district of the colony." (75) Sartorio also took the position that many Italians who became successful and moved away from the Italian colonies and acquired a totally American-style "seem either to be ashamed of their origin or afraid that people will confound them with their more ignorant countrymen; they lose all sense of responsibility toward their race and show the characteristics of the parvenu type." (76)

Things seem to have worked out better for the Italians settling in the west. Andrew Rolle, in his study, came to the conclusion that the Italians who settled in the area west of the Mississippi River found life challenging and exciting and not, as Oscar Handlin claimed, an alienating, uprooting experience. This was because the Italian immigrant in the West was able to compete on equal terms with native-born Westerners for wealth and status. They suffered little discrimination and believed that the fluid social order of the West would enable a man to go as far as his ability would enable him. Rolle's view is a reaffirmation of the Turner Thesis. (77)

The period of large Italian immigration to the United States occurred during the period of the progressive movement, but "the interaction between Italian immigration and American liberalism during the progressive era has been considered secondary in importance by historians who have focused their attention almost exclusively upon either the Italian experience or upon progressive reformism." (78)

By the 1930s there were over 1,000,000 Italians in the New York City metropolitan area, and "Little Italies" had developed near Washington Square, on Manhattan's west side, south of Fifty-Ninth Street, in East Harlem, in the area of the Bronx, between Haight and Arthur Avenues, and in South Brooklyn, Ozone Park, and Long Island City. "These 'Little Italies' took on a style of life which reflected their residents' sentiment of campanisismo, their need to live near their jobs, and the racial discrimination they encountered from non-Italians as well as from fellow countrymen. Each 'Little Italy' was in reality a conglomeration of small colonies with fellow townspeople occupying the same tenements and settling along the same streets." Many of the Italians "improvised a jargon which may be called American-Italian, a dialect as foreign to both English and Italian as any provincial dialect was distinct from the Italian language....Telephoning his wholesaler, an Italian immigrant grocer placed this order: 'Senti me wan hindi quort biff, two hemme, hiffity ponti lifi lardo.'" (79)

The composition of the various "Little Italies" was in a state of constant flux. As a family became more prosperous, it moved outside the community or into a better home within it, making room for new immigrants. "...it would be incorrect to assert that life for the Italian immigrants...was a series of endless hardships. Carefully managing their earnings, they ate well; and Italian housewives took considerable pride in providing hardy meals on a limited food budget...." (80)

For recreation Italians would, after supper, take a walk or play cards with friends. The Metropolitan Opera in New York City drew large Italian audiences when an Italian opera was being performed. Theatres, such as the Pisanelli Family Circle in San Francisco and the marionette theatre on Elizabeth Street in New York City, were also popular with Italians. (81)

Giacinto M. Serrati, editor of Il Proletario, headed the Italian Socialist Federation of North America, founded in 1902. It was formed to "focus attention upon the hardships of the Italian poor in America." Until its collapse in 1921, the Italian Socialist Federation supported the numerous strikes sponsored by the International Workers of the World (IWW). (82) In 1911, the Italian Socialist Federation affiliated with the Socialist Party of America. (83)

One of the main characteristics that the Italians had was their loyalty to their family. This loyalty brought them much criticism from Americans because many felt that this devotion to the family would not let them mix with other Americans and therefore would prevent them from becoming Americanized. Intermarriage, which was often a form of Americanization, was not that strong among the Italian immigrants. However, the South Italians have been shown to marry little outside their group, while the North Italians have been shown to marry outside their group quite extensively. (84)

The loyalty to the family and the loyalty to their village made the growth of 'Little Italies' very prominent. These "urban villages" served in a way to prevent the Italians from Americanizing as fast as some other immigrant groups. There was security and friendship in the Italian neighborhood and an immigrant was not usually prone to leave it quickly.

The Italians did not have a natural tendency for urban living. As their history shows, most Italian immigrants were peasants from agricultural areas. However, when the Italian peasants from Southern Italy started arriving in the United States in great numbers, the cities of America were growing at a fantastic pace and the city was viewed as the place of opportunity. It should be noted that many native Americans were leaving farm life for the bustle and excitement which the American city seemed to offer.

But the Italian community played an important role in the immigrant's adjustment to the United States. "The community of the immigrant generation served as a staging ground where newcomers remained until they absorbed new ideas and values that facilitated their adjustment to urban America. It thus fulfilled a vital function both for its inhabitants and for the receiving society by bridging the gap between rural traditions and the city. Italians lived and worked in this community with compatriots from all parts of the Kingdom, as well as with Irish, Germans, Poles, Scandanavians, and others; many went to church with these 'foreigners,' and their children attended the same schools. In contrast to the homeland tradition of seeking a spouse from the same place of birth, they began to intermarry with 'outsiders' from elsewhere in Italy. (85)

All in all, the Italians adapted to the life in urban America. A farm person became a city dweller and in many cases he did well. Though in the cities, the Italian immigrant often suffered from discrimination, he did not let it get the best of him. He came, he settled, he accomplished, and gradually many of the Italians, as their economic and social positions improved over generations, moved out of their initial areas of settlement. Of course, due to the close relationship of family and village, many Italians remained in their areas of prime settlement longer than other ethnic groups deemed necessary.

The Italian migration was a proletarian movement. It included peasants, landless laborers, construction workers and a small number of professional people. It started as Italian laborers followed the British and the French into North Africa and made Tunis, for example, more Italian than French. The Italians worked on the railroads and tunnels of Europe, they worked on the first Assuan Dam, the Suez Canal, the railways and ports of Tunis and Algeria. They migrated to North Africa as stonecutters, masons and unskilled workers, but they stayed and eventually became merchants, professional people and farmers. (86)

Italian migration to the United States was not heavy until after 1870. However, during the 1850s in California, trade and transportation were the only fields in which Italians accounted for over 1% of the workers. By 1870, however, agriculture and mining together accounted for more than 50% of working Italians. In the separate job categories, Italians were chiefly miners, agricultural laborers, fishermen, traders, dealers, hucksters, and peddlers. (87)

Merchants and retailers were also to be found among New York City's Italian community by the Civil War, but were outnumbered by Italian tailors, barbers, hairdressers, and laborers. As in Chicago, many Italians were artisans, and served as manufacturers of plaster images, interior decorators, cabinetmakers, bakers, carpenters, painters, stonecutters, and musical-instrument makers. New York, unlike Chicago, had a large number of the famous Italian organ-grinders. Most numerous of all occupations "were the 160 professionals, the artists and musicians, who accounted for about one-third of the gainfully employed Italians in the city." (88)

In the early 1870s the agents of various steamship companies and 'padrone' scoured the Italian countryside for manpower to emigrate to the United States where there was plenty of employment. The 'padrone' was the Italian labor boss who was in charge of the Italian workmen when they came here; the 'padrone' obtained jobs for the workmen by contract and received money from both the men and the employer. "Serving industry, but motivated by the desire for an individual profit, was the 'padrone.' Such a man established a network of personal contacts in his own country, recruited workers who bound themselves to him for a year, advanced their passage money for America, and secured it by having their fathers or other relatives give him a mortgage on their property, for a much larger sum. The system was to be found, late in the nineteenth century, in Italy and Greece." (89)

The Italian immigrant who came to the United States from South Italy was quite poor. Between 1899 and 1910 their declarations of resources to immigration officials at Ellis Island averaged less than twenty-five dollars. (90) Seventy-five percent of emigrating Italians had previously worked as farmers or in vineyards, less than 20% found similar employment in the United States, the remaining percent worked in shoe factories, glue and paint works, silk mills, machine shops, glass works, iron and coal mines, stone quarries, refineries, digging subways, constructing railroads and waterways, shoemakers, and tailors were among the leaders in the trades. (91) At the time of Mangano's writing, in Philadelphia the Italians comprised virtually all of the street cleaning force; in Chicago and Kansas City they dominated the workers in the stockyards; and in San Francisco the Italians dominated the fruit and wine business. (92)

At the time of Mangano's writings (1917), he found that in New York City alone the Italian professionals found numbered several hundred practicing attorneys, over 250 physicians, many bankers and businessmen. (93) Mangano also found that Italian unskilled labor averaged between $7 and $10 per week. He also found that the majority of Italian families living in cities lived on $10 to $16 a week. (94)

Though times were not very good for the Italian in the United States, he was better off than in Italy. As mentioned previously, Italians were mostly laborers.

What is peculiar in the Italian continent can be brought out by some simple comparisons. In 1907, for example (a year when the immigration from all countries was very heavy, and when that from Italy was one-fourth of the total, and when Italian skilled workers were a fifth of all skilled immigrants), Italian plumbers were one in 150 arriving plumbers, locksmiths one in 74 of their kind, milliners one in 48, painters and glaziers one in 16, clerks and accountants one in 23, plasterers one in 26, saddlers one in 18, machinists one in 38, tailors one in 8. Extremely few, likewise, were the butchers, bookbinders, iron and steel and other metal workers, hat makers, woodworkers, and wheelwrights. And generally these immigrants originated in North Italy. In a different group of occupations, the Italians have been much more numerous. Of blacksmiths, bakers, millers, in some years miners, their representation has been near the average for all peoples. It fell but little below such an average in 1907 in the case of cabinetmakers, carpenters, dressmakers, gardeners, and metal workers (other than in iron and steel), but in some years has exceeded the average. (95)

The Italian immigrant also had high representation as stonecutters, mechanics, mariners, masons, barbers, seamstresses and shoemakers. In most cases, during the first two decades of the twentieth century, one-half or more of all arriving masons were Italian and in some years a third to a half of all the stonecutters were from Italy. (96)

Italian fishermen often made up one-half of immigrants who were fishermen. (97) The Italians also were among the most numerous of bootblacks. Foerster elaborated: "The bootblacks, humblest of all, have not, saving in rare instances, plied their trade in Italy. But they found it open to them here (or occupied mainly by negroes) and they brought to it a pride in neat work which is in some sense a national attribute. In goodly numbers they entered the trade very early, at the time in fact when the street musicians, with their bears and monkeys, and ragpickers, were still the conspicuous types; and they were one in sixteen of all bootblacks counted five years after the Civil War had ended. Twenty years later, in those quarters of New York where the foreign population dwelt, 473 out of the 474 foreign bootblacks enumerated were Italians--and the native workers numbered 10!" (98) Many Italian immigrants became barbers, hairdressers, and shoemakers. (99) The Italian immigrant also was prominent as dealers in groceries, wines, liquors, and other goods. In 1870 the Italian consul-general estimated that three out of five of all street sellers of peaches, pears, apples and chestnuts in New York City were Italians. (100) "In 1892 the consul-general in New York reported to his government that Italians owned most of the fruit stands in the metropolis and ran them profitably; in Boston also were many. In the Far West, during the period of gold excitement, the dealers had more success trading in the camps than their brethren had digging in the mines. Subsequently they rose to considerable importance in San Francisco and elsewhere in the coast states, selling wine and liquors, groceries, fruits, and vegetables.... In New Orleans, long a center for trade with Sicily, the Sicilians had achieved a leading position in the sale of fruit, vegetables, and oysters." (101)

Many Italian businessmen made their living dealing in the Italian communities and serving the needs of their fellow Italians. The Italians wanted to enter business very badly. "The tremendous increment of the immigrant population since 1900, all unmeasured statistically as to cooperation, has certainly boosted the Italian participation in trade. For we must remember that many general laborers, miners, and others are tempted to enter 'bisinisse,' and that they can do so by learning fifty words of English and buying a fruit stand. Sometimes a wife manages a shop or stand while the husband continues at his work. In New York many men have begun with a pushcart, then got the privilege of a stand, then a concession to sell garden produce in connection with a grocery store, and finally have set up a shop of their own. In small towns and at railroad stations many Italian fruit stands are now to be found. The Italians' love of their trade, bringing an eagerness to have fresh fruits and to display them in comely arrangements, has undoubtedly somewhat stimulated the fruit consumption of the American people. A common type in our foreign communities is the coal and wood or coal and ice dealer, observed half a century ago in San Francisco. In some places he has been the successor of the Jews, as these have succeeded the Irish. The business is simple enough: one rents an unused basement, constructs crudely in the rear a bin or bunk, then hangs out a sign or peddles small portions in the tenements." (102)

By 1870, one-seventh of the Italian workers were general laborers, and by 1890 more than a third of all Italian workers were general laborers. (103)

The Immigration Commission (Dillingham Commission) meeting between 1907-1910 studied the economic condition of the Italian immigrants. The Commission found that the South Italians had the largest portion of men in the U.S. less than five years among the immigrants working in the coal fields of the Southwest. (104)

The Italians coming at the present time are mostly direct from Europe, while those brought in during the early days were from other states of this country. Many leave each year, but the percentage of those coming in is much larger than of those going out, and a considerable number are making Oklahoma their permanent home. From information secured from steamship agents, it is estimated that during the year 1908, about 458 went to Italy. Out of this number about 800, making a gain of 575 in the Italian popu- lation for the past year.
At the present time Italians are found in every town and mining camp in the coal fields, and the number is about equally divided between North and South Italians. More property is owned by these races than by any other immigrants, and in each community they are prospering. In all cases they have gone to work in the coal mines, and those now in business were formerly miners. It is estimated that there are about 10,000 in the coal regions and that this number will be greatly increased during the next few years. (105)

The Dillingham Commission went on to find that in 1890 the Italians were not very numerous in the iron and steel industry in the United States. They had 442 workers out of a total number of 57,793. (106) They also found that the

Italians showed a tendency to enter the slaughtering and meat packing industry shortly after arriving in the United States. (107) Italians were not very prominent in the glass blowing industry in the United States with only 391 workers out of a total of 47,378 in 1900. (108) The Italians had a fair amount of representation in the cigar and tobacco manufacturing industry with 2,032 workers out of a United States total of 131,464. (109)

The Dillingham Commission found that the literacy of the Italian mine workers was that of the Northern Italians, 82.8% could read and 76.9% could write; while among the South Italians 59.7% could read and also 59.7% could write. (110) This low rate of literacy contributed to the Italian mine workers being abused and taken advantage of in many different ways. (111)

Many Italians went into the manufacturing and dyeing of silk goods. The story of the Italians in Paterson, New Jersey is an interesting case in point. The immigration of Italians into Paterson began when a few families of fruit vendors took up residence in the city a short time after the Civil War. Around 1880-1885 the first Italian workmen came to Paterson and found employment in public works and in the constructing of street railways. Most of the early Italian immigrants left Paterson after the railway construction was completed. Others eventually went to work in the dyehouses. This was the start of Italian employment in the silk industry. Between 1888 and 1890 the dye workers of Paterson participated in a number of strikes. At the time the dye workers were mostly English or American, with some Germans, Scotch, Irish and Frenchmen among them. The work in the dyehouses was difficult and grimy and the men struck for higher wages. In order to break the strike, one of the dyemakers hired Italian immigrants and used them as strikebreakers. From this time, until 1903-1904, large numbers of Italians were brought into the city of Paterson and by the end of the first decade of the twentieth century, the silk industry in Paterson was almost entirely composed of Italians. Before the "dyers' strike," few Italians had been employed in the Paterson silk mills. However, as more and more Italians began working in the Paterson silk mills they encouraged their friends and relatives to come to America and settle in Paterson, New Jersey. The silk manufacturers of Paterson also encouraged Italians to settle in the area and work in the mills. The vast increase of Italian workers in the silk industry dates from 1896-97. Following this date the silk industry grew very rapidly and Italians were hired in order to meet the extra labor demands. The English-speaking workers were replaced by the Italians and as other lines of work opened up, many of the English-speaking workers left the silk industry. At the end of the first decade of the twentieth century the great majority of the Italian population living in Paterson, New Jersey was dependent upon the silk industry for their livelihood. The majority of the silk workers in Paterson were from northern Italy and among the southern Italians only a few of them were Sicilians. The immigration of Italians was slowed by the financial depression in 1907 and immigration of Italians to Paterson was also slowed by the entrance of Russian Jews into the area. (112)

Conditions of the Italian workmen in construction crews were generally very poor. (113) The Dillingham Commission reported: "The standard of living in construction camps is necessarily below that which surrounds industries offering more permanent employment and facilities for women. Many of the immigrants employed in such work, having come direct from their homes in Europe to the construction camps, have to be taught by their friends already on the work how to cook. Wherever there is a woman in the house there is a marked difference in the appearance as to cleanliness. In most of the construction camps there are practically no women. Such is usually the case on railroad construction." (114)

Of the amount of construction workers in the East, at the time of the Commission study, the Italians made up 47% of which the South Italians constituted 32.2%. (115) The Dillingham Commission also reported that of the Italian male employees who had been in the United States less than five years, none earned as much as $3.50 a day, with the exception of the North Italians, of whom less than one percent of them earned between $3.50 and $4.00 per day. Also reported that of the North Italians, 55.5% earned less than $1.50 per day, while the proportions for the South Italians was almost the same. (116)

"A padrone, having once established himself with a contractor, usually remains with him enlarging his business and increasing the number of his commissions as the contractor's business grows. The contractors employing a large number of men like the arrangement, as it insures them labor, does away with the necessity of keeping an interpreter, and gives them, through the padrone, a hold on the men that they would not otherwise have. This system prevailed in all except five of the camps studied in the East, these five being camps that had a large percentage of other than Italian laborers. One case was noted where two padrones operated a bank and labor agency in Philadelphia and a string of commissary stores on the railroad work in New Jersey. One padrone remained at the scene of the construction work, directing the commissaries, while his banking partner in Philadelphia gathered the men and sent them out. They also handled the savings of the laborers whom they employed." (117)

"On all the work connected with the New York City reservoir and aqueduct construction there were regular police furnished by the city. In one camp there were about 20 of the contractor's men vested with the authority of a sheriff, in addition to the city police. With this force of officers there was no trouble in keeping order. In some of the outlying camps the walking bosses maintain order, although the work is patrolled by the city police. On all railroad work it is the custom for the camp superintendent or walking bosses to maintain order. Where the padrones have charge of all the commissions, as is the case on nearly all of the work covered by this report, they are looked to by the contractors to keep order in the camp. When a disturbance in camp occurs the padrone or foreman holds the men he deems best arrested until the local authorities can be notified. The most unusual cause for calling on these local authorities is found in connection with a strike." (118)

In the cotton mills the employees rated the various groups employed by them in descending order:

In Fall River and New Bedford, Massachusetts:

1. General efficiency - American, English and Irish, French Canadian, North Italian, Portuguese, Polish, South Italian, Syrian.

2. Progress - Same as above.

3. Adaptability - American, English, Irish, French Canadian, North Italian, South Italian, Portuguese, Syrian and Polish.

4. Tractability - Portuguese, French Canadian, North Italian, American, Irish, English, Polish, Syrian and South Italian.

5. Industriousness - Portuguese, French Canadian, North Italian, American, English, Irish, Polish, South Italian, Syrian. (119)

81

Beck, in his study of the Italian in Chicago during the early part of the twentieth century, observed that wages for Italian women were about average for the cities' female workers. The starting salary for those in the clothing industry was $7-$9 per week. Machine operators had the possibility of eventually earning up to $38 per week. Department store workers earned between $9 and $25 per week. But Beck also pointed out that Italian women employed in the stockyards earned less than half of the average group. (120) Beck also stated that "While the number of young girls and women employed in industry is very small, the heads of the employment departments consulted all bore testimony as to the industry and trustworthiness of Italian girls and women and wished that more could be secured for their respective concerns." (121)

In his search, Beck also found that the Italians spent a smaller percentage of income on clothing than any other foreign-speaking group in Chicago. Much clothing was bought second hand and received from charities for nothing. The Italians used the free clinics run by charities and the city of Chicago a great deal. In the area of fraternal and benefit insurance, Beck found that the Italians spent more per capita on this than any other group in Chicago. He also found that, except for gambling, the Italians spent less proportionately on recreation than any other group in Chicago. He also stated that many Italians worked six days a week during the summer and saved the wages of three, "...which insures them a living during the unemployment months." Beck found that more Italians were purchasing their own homes, which attested to the fact of their thrift. "As no other group in Chicago, they have created their wealth by the sweat of their brow." (122)

Among the Italians, the father often attempted to raise himself financially by buying a tenement house and would use all the members of his family as employees so that he could pay off the mortgage. An Italian father, in his early thirties, went to Hull-House in grief because of the death of his daughter who was only twelve years old. "She was the oldest kid I had," he exclaimed. "Now I shall have to go back to work again until the next one is able to take care of me." A South Italian peasant who had worked picking olives and oranges in his early childhood did not see anything wrong with using child labor and he did not notice that he worked under better conditions in Italy than his children did in the United States. (123)

Italians from Northern Italy founded Chicago's Italian community and dominated the settlement until the 1880s. "The men generally worked at skilled and semi-skilled jobs, or found employment in service and trade occupations. They became saloonkeepers and bartenders; fruit, candy and ice cream vendors; confectioners; clerks; barbers; hairdressers; and restaurant owners or employees." (124) The mainly unskilled labor that later became associated with the capabilities and training of the Italians was formerly dominated by the Germans, Irish and the Swedes. (125) The Southern Italians had it quite difficult in the city of Chicago, for when they came to Chicago they "generally understood little about the English language. They also lacked contacts with potential American employers, and knew nothing concerning American labor practices. To compensate for these deficiencies they looked for an intermediary--someone who spoke both languages, understood old-world traditions and new-world business operations, and could get in touch with American employers who needed unskilled workers. This intermediary was the padrone, or labor boss." (126)

Professor Humbert Nelli points out that "Few Americans doubted that padroni operated among unskilled immigrant labor and especially among 'Southerners' in the United States. Disagreement arose over the composition of the padrone groups, its size, and when it operated. Available evidence suggests that a formal contract labor system did exist on a limited scale before the Foran Act in 1885 forbade it, and that this system involved women and children as well as adult males. After 1885 the padrone acted merely as a private labor agent, owning neither license nor office. Probably most padroni fulfilled only this function before, as well as after, the mid-1880s." (127) The padroni or boss met the immigrants at the railroad stations or at the docks and promised steady work and good wages. Some of the Italian immigrants did not bow to the pressures of the padroni immediately, but in the Italian sections of the large American cities the newcomers were constantly bombarded by padroni pressures which were intended to recruit their services for the boss. The padroni knew various employers, spoke English and Italian and understood American labor practices. Because of this he had authority over the recent Italian immigrant and was important to the American businessman. The bosses directed the Italian laborers to different parts of the United States and into Canada to work on the railroads and on various construction jobs. "Chicago became an important padrone stronghold, partly because of the city's position as a railroad center and partly because of its geographical location. Railroad and other construction jobs tended to be seasonal, and Chicago served as a clearing house for seasonal workers on the entire country as well as the Middle East." (128)

Italian immigrants also went out to the Far West to make their homes and their livelihood. It was in the area of agriculture that the Italians in California flourished. They applied Old World care and New World methods to viniculture and viticulture and were very successful. Beginning in the 1880s, North Italians from Genoa, Turin and various Lombard vineyard towns came to California vineyards in appreciable numbers. In 1881, Andrea Sbarboro, a Genoese banker, interested some of the Italian peasants living in California in settling cooperatively on fifteen hundred acres of land at Asti, near Cloverdale. "In company with chemists, Pietro C. Rossi, who became his winemaker, founded the Italian-Swiss Agricultural Colony in the Sonoma Valley." After a few difficult years, this colony, with its five thousand acres of land, flourished. "By 1911 the Italian-Swiss Colony won the highest award ever given American champagne - the Grand Prix of the Turin International Exposition for its 'Golden State Extra Dry.' By shipping railroad tank cars full of wine eastward, the colony came to control much of the United States wine market." (129) The success of many Italians in the West caused the Italian Consul-General to report that the central and western states got the 'better element' of the Italian immigrants. (130)

In the northern states, Italians worked largely on the railroad and construction gangs; in the South they worked in phosphate mines, as cotton pickers and mill hands. Later they went to labor in the isolated construction sites of the United States and Canada. (131)

It was reported that, at the time, out of every 100 Italian workers discharged--40% returned to Italy, 10% remained in assigned localities, and 50% went to the nearest city. Eventually a degree of permanence resulted from the stable positions in industry gained by the Italian male, who may then have established residence and brought their families to America. World War I also played a large part in stopping the "birds of passage" movement. (132)

Italians were numerous in "foundries, automobile factories, manufactories of cutlery and fixtures. They work in the lumber mills of the South and California, paper and wood pulp, rubber, glass, tobacco, oil and chemical, shoe and textile (except cotton) factories. They have invaded the clothing industry, rivaling the Jews since 1890 in New York and Philadelphia....They are in the glove, knit goods, button and artificial flower trades; in candy, paper box, celluloid, and piano making; in laundries and canneries." (133)

Philip Rose, in his research, found that a small percentage of Italians went into farming in America. He attributed this to "the remembrance of former bitter experience in agriculture in Italy; the clinging to urban life as it was known there, and corresponding distaste for the solitude of the American farm; and the quick returns from industrial work as compared with the hard labor and slow returns of the farm." (134)

Agricultural settlements were established by construction workers who remained close to the previous site, who bought and cultivated the land; by groups temporarily cultivating tobacco or sugar cane, by berry and hops pickers, or those who canned fruits and vegetables seasonally and remain --all of whom were from the city; and by predominantly Southern Italians, who were market gardeners that acquired a piece of land outside the city. Northern Italians participated where union leadership was involved, such as in Vineland, New Jersey; Glastonbury, Connecticut; Tontitown, Arkansas; Valdise, North Carolina; and Asti, California. These agricultural settlements were not made up of diversified farmers, or staple producers. They lacked technical know-how, and their shortage of capital obstructed them from crop rotation. (135) However, the Italians were in general successful truck farmers. (136)

Life was so difficult for the Italian immigrant workers, that Sartorio commented, "They perform the duties that the slaves performed in ancient Rome; they sweep the streets, black shoes, build railroads, dig in mines, do the rougher work in factories. The more thrifty succeed in a few years in opening a grocery store or a saloon. They are located from the rest of the world by what I may call the instinct of self-preservation; they know that as soon as they step outside of the Italian colony they are almost as helpless as babies, owing to their lack of knowledge of the language, customs, and laws of this country. This is one of the fundamental reasons why these people who, through generations have been in touch with nature, living in the open air, working in the fields, prefer the gray life of the slums: anything rather than to be separated from their countrymen." (137)

The work of unskilled occupations such as mines, railroads, general construction was so hazardous and so many Italians were being killed doing this type of work that the Italian government directed its consuls in the United States to investigate. (138)   Many Italians stayed working in difficult occupations and working under hazardous conditions.   But many Italians saved a good percentage of their earnings and invested it in business once they had saved enough capital.

In the first two decades of the twentieth century, the Italian professional class in America consisted mostly of physicians, dentists, and lawyers.   Most were mediocre, and few achieved any sort of eminence in their field.   Those educated in America usually attended second-rate professional schools. (139)

The Italians have in general been viewed with favor by the employing classes.   This was in part because they were very hard workers and worked in poor conditions.   They have also been often used as strike breakers such as the Pennsylvania coal strike of 1887-88.   "A few took employment during the longshoremen's strike of 1887, and their increasing numbers became the employers' means of preventing further trouble.   The immediate cause of the introduction of Italians into the New York clothing industry is declared to have been the employers' desire to escape trade-union demands.   With other workers, they helped to break the meat packing strike in 1904." (140)   Also in 1909, while many of the non-Italian workers in the New York City garment industry went out on strike for a three month period, the Italian women remained at their posts and additional hundreds of them came to work to fill the vacated spaces of the non-Italian workers. (141)   The organizer of the Ladies' Garment Workers Union in Cleveland also complained that at the meeting of the local, the turnout of Italian girls was very small. (142)   However, though only a small proportion of Italians joined unions, the Italian soon started to participate in unions with greater gusto.

To some extent the Italian's eyes have been opened to the effect of his actions.   Where the existing unions have been strong, he has been ready to enter them; so in some of the mines, so too, in certain quarters, in the building trades--and one son of Italy has risen to important office in the International Hodcarriers' Union.   In the anthracite strikes of 1900 and 1902 the Italians were won to participation; their leaders, the Irish, in actually overcoming for the time their regional factionalism, did what the Italians themselves and their employers had often failed to accomplish.   In 1907, in New York, six thousand organized longshore-men and many others who were unorganized played an important role in a great six weeks' strike which involved thirty thousand workers; as it happened, the strike failed and keen resentment at the union was felt. Under American or English-speaking leaders, the bituminous coal miners of a portion of the western Pennsylvania fields struck for sixteen months, beginning in 1910; but again discouragement over the failure of their efforts was acute. Upon many counts memorable, a strike was started by Poles and Italians in the textile mills of Lawrence in 1912; the conditions protested were not unlike those in innumerable immigrant occupations, but the publicity given them stirred much of that general sympathy which became a factor in a settlement favorable to the workers. In this strike, the Italian and Poles were the most active belligerents and to an exceptional extent did the picketing. Though most of the leaders were English-speaking, one Italian organized the strike for the quasi-syndicalist Industrial Workers of the World, which in other centers also has found support among his countrymen. During the war years, with the tremendous enhancement of the bargaining power of labor, Italians have frequently participated in strikes and at times, as in the case of the coal heavers of the New York piers in 1917, they were the first to quit work. (143)

The strike by the United Mine Workers in Colorado in 1902 was participated in by many Italian workers. As a result of the strike 98 men were deported, most of them Italian. The National Guard had been sent in by Governor James H. Peabody, and their commander exercised his discretion over those Italian and others who he considered to be agitators and troublemakers and responsible for the outbreak of 'lawlessness.' By mid-April, 1904, all but the Italians had returned to work. (144)

The strike in 1910 against Chicago's clothing manufacturers saw 40,000 workers go on strike. One-quarter of them were Italian. The strike failed, but led to the founding of the Amalgamated Clothing Workers of America, "which by the end of the decade had succeeded in completing the organization of Chicago's garment workers and in establishing standard wages, hours, and shop conditions in the industry." (145)

Most Italians involved in strikes were not unionized at first, and their "grievances were locally inspired." The "epidemic" of strikes throughout New York State in 1913 "appeared to be the result of an abortive attempt to found an Italian national union, variously known as The International Laborers' Union, The General Laborers' International Union, and The Laborers' Union." Its headquarters were located in Mount Vernon, New York, and its leader was Felix D'Alessandro. The organization had 223 locals and 72,000 members. It sought to gain for its members, a 25¢ minimum wage, an 8-hour day, and time-and-a-half for overtime, nights, Sundays and holidays. (146)

In speaking of progressivism, the historian Eric Goldman suggests that identification with one's minority served as a divisive factor among labor, rendering them more susceptible to the designs of their employers. In a 1919 U.S. Steel Corporation strike, the employers gave these typical instructions, "We want you to stir up as much bad feeling as you possibly can between the Serbians and the Italians....Call up every question you can in reference to racial hatred between these two nationalities." (147)

Of the more recent Italian-American labor leaders, the late Luigi Antonini and Anthony Scotto were among the most successful. Luigi Antonini "gained prominence as a convincing spokesman in the general strike of the waistmakers in 1913 and soon after began to organize the Italian-American garment workers." Antonini helped establish Local 89, which became the largest in the ILGWU (International Ladies' Garment Workers Union). He became state chairman of the American Labor Party, and in 1940 was a presidential elector. When the American Labor Party became infiltrated with Communists, he helped establish the Liberal Party. In 1951, he was a delegate of the A.F. of L. at the World Congress of International Confederation of Free Trade Unions in Milan. (148)

Anthony Scotto was president of Local 1814 of the International Longshoremen's Association. He was a combination of an old time rough boss with a mixture of sophistication. "Exercising exceptional vision and pluck, he has used his position to oppose welfare cuts and back civil rights, urban renewal, voter registration, and the re-election of a liberal mayor, John V. Lindsay, who was not supposed to appeal to the Italo-American working class. As if to refute charges of Mafia ties, one of the first actions Scotto took as manager of a country club in New Jersey was to exclude known gangsters from membership." (149)

Since coming to this country, many Italians have been very successful in the fields of popular music, theatre, opera, orchestras, art, architecture, sculpture and sports. (150) However, this is a small percentage of the total Italian population.

Source Notes

(1) Philip M. Rose, The Italian in America (New York: George H. Doran Co., 1922), pp. 18-19.

(2) Robert F. Foerster, The Italian Emigration of Our Times (New York: Russell and Russell, 1968), p. 51. This book was first published in 1919.

(3) Ibid., p. 50.

(4) Luciano J. Iorizzo and Salvatore Mondello, The Italian-Americans (New York: Twayne Publishers, Inc., 1971), pp. 3-4.

(5) Foerster, op. cit., pp. 320-324.

(6) Rose, op. cit., p. 27.

(7) Philip Taylor, The Distant Magnet: European Migration to the U.S.A. (New York: Harper & Row Publishers, 1971), p. 45.

(8) Ibid., p. 51. The source that Taylor refers to is the Cambridge Economic History of Europe, VI.

(9) 52 Congress I Session, House Miscellaneous Documents, 19 & 20, 211.

(10) Iorizzo and Mondello, op. cit., pp. 44-45.

(11) Taylor, op. cit., p. 98.

(12) Frederick Jackson Turner, The Frontier in American History (New York: Henry Holt and Company, 1953), p. 264. This book was first published in 1920.

(13) Andrew J. Torrielli, Italian Opinion on America, as Revealed by Italian Travelers, 1850-1900 (Cambridge, Mass.: Harvard University Press, 1941), pp. 3-38.

(14) Andrew F. Rolle, The Immigrant Upraised (Norman, Oklahoma: The University of Oklahoma Press, 1968), p. 21.

(15) New York Times, March 23, 1880, p. 4.

(16) New York Times, December 29, 1880, p. 2.

(17) Josh Foster Carr, "The Coming of the Italians," Outlook,
      LXXXII (1906), 420.

(18) Oscar Handlin, The Uprooted (New York: Grosset and
      Dunlop, Publishers, 1951), p. 53.

(19) Merle Curti and Kendall Birr, "The Immigrant and the
      American Image in Europe, 1860-1914," The
      Mississippi Valley Historical Review, XXXVII, 2
      (September, 1950), 211.

(20) Ibid., p. 218.

(21) Gerald Shaughnessy, Has the Immigrant Kept the Faith?
      (New York: The Macmillan Company, 1925), pp.
      149-180.

(22) Taylor, op. cit., p. 105.

(23) Shaughnessy, op. cit., p. 86.

(24) Reports of the Immigration Commission, 1907-1910, 41
      vols. (Washington, D.C.: Government Printing
      Office, 1911) Vol. 4, p. 84.

(25) Ibid.

(26) Ibid., pp. 84-85.

(27) Immigration and Emigration (Washington, D.C.: Bureau
      of Labor Statistics, Government Printing Office,
      1915), p. 1099.

(28) Shaughnessy, op. cit., pp. 175, 180.

(29) Joseph Lopreato, Peasants No More (San Francisco:
      Chandler Publishing Co., 1967), p. 43.

(30) Shaughnessy, op. cit., pp. 139-180 and Historical Stat-
      istics of the United States (Washington, D.C.:
      Government Printing Office, 1945), pp. 33-35.

(31) New York Times, March 4, 1880, p. 2.

(32) Iorizzo and Mondello, op. cit., pp. 5-6.

(33) Taylor, op. cit., pp. 149-150.

(34) Ibid., p. 162.

(35) Humbert S. Nelli, "Ethnic Group Assimilation: The Italian Experience," Cities in American History, ed. Kenneth T. Jackson and Stanley K. Schultz (New York: Alfred A. Knopf, 1972), 199.

(36) J. Joseph Hutchmacher, A Nation of Newcomers: Ethnic Minority Groups in American History (New York: Dell Publishing Co., Inc., 1967), p. 32.

(37) Rose, op. cit., pp. 53-54.

(38) U.S. Industrial Commission, Reports of the Industrial Commission on Immigration, Vol. XV (Washington: Government Printing Office, 1901), p. LXVII.

(39) Charles W. Coulter, The Italians of Cleveland (Cleveland: Cleveland Americanization Committee, 1919), p. 8.

(40) Ibid., pp. 8-9.

(41) Nelli, op. cit., pp. 199-200. For a greater in depth study of the pattern of Italian settlement in Chicago see Humbert S. Nelli, The Italians in Chicago, 1880-1930 (New York: Oxford University Press, 1970), pp. 22-54.

(42) Charlotte Adams, "Italian Life in New York," Harper's Magazine LXII (April, 1881), 676.

(43) I.W. Horweth, "Are the Italians a Dangerous Class?" Charities Review IV (November, 1894), 38.

(44) Alberto Pecorini, "The Italians in the United States," Forum XLV (January, 1911), 17.

(45) Ibid.

(46) G. LaPiana, The Italians in Milwaukee (Milwaukee, Associated Charities of Milwaukee, 1915), p. 14.

(47) Ibid., p. 16.

(48) Ibid., p. 18.

(49) Rose, op. cit., p. 67.

(50) Ibid., p. 68.

(51) Foerster, op. cit., pp. 325-326.

(52) John Foster Carr, op. cit., pp. 428-429.

(53) Jacob A. Riis, How the Other Half Lives (New York: Charles Scribner's Sons, 1890), p. 52.

(54) Lawrence Frank Pisani, The Italian in America (New York: Exposition Press, 1957), pp. 69-70.

(55) Reports of the Immigration Commission, 1907-1910, 41 vols. (Washington, D.C.: Government Printing Office, 1911) I, p. 35.

(56) Ibid., p. 36.

(57) Ibid., p. 37.

(58) Nathan Glazer and Daniel Patrick Moynihan, Beyond the Melting Pot (Cambridge, Mass.: The M.I.T. Press, 1963), p. 186.

(59) Ibid., p. 187. For an interesting study of LaGuardia see Arthur Mann, LaGuardia Comes to Power, 1933, (New York: J.B. Lippincott Company, 1965). For a study of Vito Marcantonio see John GaGumia, Vito Marcantonio, The People's Politician, (Dubuque: Kendall-Hunt, 1969).

(60) Ibid.

(61) Humbert S. Nelli, "Italians in Urban America: A Study in Ethnic Adjustment," International Migration Review, Vol. I, No. 3 (Summer, 1967), 40-41. For a more in depth study of Nelli's position see Humbert S. Nelli, The Italians in Chicago, 1880-1930, op. cit.

(62) Gilbert Osofsky, Harlem: The Making of a Ghetto (New York: Harper & Row Publishers, 1968), pp. 127-128.

(63)   Herbert Gans, The Urban Villagers (Glencoe, Illinois:
        The Free Press, 1962), passim.

(64)   Antonio Mangano, Sons of Italy: A Social and Religious
        Study of the Italians in America (New York:
        Missionary Education Movement of the United States
        and Canada, 1919), pp. 26-29.

(65)   Ibid., pp. 102-103.

(66)   Frank Orman Beck, The Italian in Chicago (Chicago:
        Chicago Department of Public Welfare Bulletin), no
        date, p. 5.

(67)   Ibid., pp. 5-16.

(68)   Ibid., p. 17.

(69)   Ibid., p. 18.

(70)   Ibid., p. 25.

(71)   Reports of the Immigration Commission, 1907-1910, op.
        cit., XXVI, p. 6.

(72)   Nelli, The Italians in Chicago, 1880-1930, op. cit.,
        pp. 13-14.

(73)   Enrico C. Sartorio, Social and Religious Life of Italians
        in America (Boston: The Christopher Publishing
        House, 1918), p. 21.

(74)   Ibid., p. 23.

(75)   Ibid., p. 19.

(76)   Ibid., p. 44.

(77)   Rolle, op. cit., passim.

(78)   Iorizzo and Mondello, op. cit., p. 87.

(79)   Ibid., p. 88.

(80)   Ibid., pp. 90-91.

(81)   Ibid., p. 91.

(82) Ibid., p. 94.

(83) David A. Shannon, The Socialist Party of America (Chicago: Quadrangle Books, 1967), p. 44.

(84) Julius Drachsler, Intermarriage in New York City (New York: Columbia University Press, 1921), pp. 66-70.

(85) Nelli, "Ethnic Group Assimilation: The Italian Experience," op. cit., p. 200.

(86) Glazer and Moynihan, op. cit., p. 182.

(87) Iorizzo and Mondello, op. cit., p. 13.

(88) Ibid., pp. 13-14.

(89) Taylor, op. cit., p. 13.

(90) 61 Congress, 3 session, Senate Documents 756, 349, 358.

(91) Mangano, op. cit., p. 21.

(92) Ibid., p. 22.

(93) Ibid.

(94) Ibid., pp. 22-23.

(95) Foerster, op. cit., p. 332.

(96) Ibid., p. 333.

(97) Ibid.

(98) Ibid., pp. 334-335.

(99) Ibid., pp. 335-337.

(100) Ibid., p. 337.

(101) Ibid., p. 337.

(102) Ibid., pp. 337-338.

(103) Ibid., p. 343.

(104) Reports of the Immigration Commission, 1907-1910, 41 vols. Vol. 7 (Washington, D.C.: Government Printing Office, 1911), p. 12.

(105) Ibid., p. 17.

(106) Reports of the Immigration Commission, 1907-1910. Vol. 8, p. 22.

(107) Reports of the Immigration Commission, 1907-1910. Vol. 13, p. 26.

(108) Reports of the Immigration Commission, 1907-1910. Vol. 14, p. 24.

(109) Reports of the Immigration Commission, 1907-1910. Vol. 15, p. 24.

(110) Reports of the Immigration Commission, 1907-1910. Vol. 16, p. 361.

(111) For a good example of this see Gino C. Speranza, "The Italian Foreman as a Social Agent," Charities XI (July 4, 1903), 26-28.

(112) Reports of the Immigration Commission, 1907-1910. Vol. 11, pp. 18-19.

(113) See Dominic T. Ciolli, "The 'Wop' in the Track Gang," Immigration in America Review, (July, 1916), 61-64. In this article the author tells of the terrible conditions of the Italian laborer working for the railroad.

(114) Reports of the Immigration Commission, 1907-1910. Vol. 19, p. 396.

(115) Ibid., p. 388.

(116) Ibid., p. 392.

(117) Ibid., pp. 393-394.

(118) Ibid., p. 401.

(119) Reports of the Immigration Commission, 1907-1910. Vol. 10, p. 179.

(120) Beck, op. cit., pp. 9-10.

(121) Ibid., p. 10.

(122) Ibid., p. 12.

(123) Ray Ginger, Altgeld's America: The London Ideal Versus Changing Relations (Chicago: Quandrangle Books, Inc., 1965), pp. 30-31.

(124) Nelli, The Italians in Chicago, 1880-1930, op. cit., p. 22.

(125) Ibid., p. 55.

(126) Ibid., p. 56.

(127) Ibid., p. 57.

(128) Ibid., pp. 58-59.

(129) Rolle, op. cit., pp. 266-267.

(130) "Immigrants From Italy," New York Times, Oct. 6, 1895, p. 25.

(131) Rose, op. cit., p. 55.

(132) Ibid., p. 55.

(133) Ibid., p. 56.

(134) Ibid., p. 57.

(135) Ibid., pp. 58-59.

(136) Howard Grose, Aliens or American? With introduction by Josiah Strong. (New York, Toronto: Young People's Missionary Movement, 1906), pp. 147-148.

(137) Sartorio, op. cit., pp. 18-19.

(138) Ibid., p. 28.

(139) Ibid., p. 41.

(140) Foerster, op. cit., pp. 401-402.

(141) *Ibid*., p. 403.

(142) Coulter, *op*. *cit*., p. 13.

(143) Foerster, *op*. *cit*., pp. 403-404.

(144) Iorizzo and Mondello, *op*. *cit*., pp. 78-79.

(145) *Ibid*., p. 80.

(146) *Ibid*., p. 82.

(147) Eric F. Goldman, *Rendezvous With Destiny* (New York: Vintage Books, 1956), p. 235.

(148) Iorizzo and Mondello, *op*. *cit*., p. 83.

(149) *Ibid*., pp. 63-64.

(150) For further study about Italian occupations, see Adriana Spadoni, "The Italian Working Woman in New York," *Colliers*, 49, No. 1 (March 23, 1912), 14-15; and LaPiana, *op*. *cit*., pp. 7-10.